Marvin H. Meltzer

Preface by
Marvin H. Meltzer
Introduction by
Carlo Paganelli

Chief Editor of Collection
Maurizio Vitta

Publishing Coordinator
Franca Rottola

Editorial Staff
Cristina Rota

Graphic Design
Break Point

Editing and Translation
Martyn J. Anderson

Colour-separation
Litofilms Italia, Bergamo

Printing
Bolis Poligrafiche S.p.a. Bergamo

First published February 2002

Copyright 2002
by l'Arca Edizioni

All rights reserved
Printed in Italy

ISBN 88-7838-097-0

Contents

5 Preface by *Marvin H. Meltzer*
7 Interpretation is Innovation by *Carlo Paganelli*

11 **Works**
13 **DEVELOPMENT PROJECTS**
14 Hudson Street Townhouses, New York, NY
18 100 West 81st Street, New York, NY
24 Greencroft Condominiums, New Rochelle, NY
28 The Enclave, New York, NY

33 **AFFORDABLE/LOW-INCOME HOUSING**
34 Melrose Court, Bronx, NY
40 Carmen B. Bermudez Residence, Bronx, NY
44 351 East 61st Street, New York, NY
48 Gerard Court and River Court, Bronx, NY
52 Crotona Avenue Apartments, Bronx, NY
58 Jennings Street Apartments, Bronx, NY
64 Intervale Avenue Apartments, Bronx, NY
68 Bradhurst Court, New York, NY

73 **URBAN PROJECTS**
74 306–308 East 38th Street, New York, NY
78 Park Avenue Sephardic Congregation, New York, NY
84 83rd Street and York Avenue, New York, NY
88 Queens West Development Project, Long Island City, Queens, NY

96 Complete List of Works
97 Biography

Preface
by Marvin H. Meltzer

The landscape of New York City, primarily Manhattan, presents opportunities for urban architects that no other place in this country offers. Every block in this tiny, densely populated island has an identity, exuding its own character and special qualities. A journey through New York streets is full of surprises. There is always something new to see and experience, something that pleases or startles the eye; every street, every avenue presents an amazing patchwork of treasures to be discovered and, for an architect, to be reinvented. It's a marvelous environment from which to work and build a career.

I grew up in St. Paul, Minnesota. Coming to New York City—the place I now call home—was, and still is, an eye-opening experience. In 1961, after graduating from the University of Minnesota, I was drafted into military service and eventually stationed on Governor's Island, off the tip of lower Manhattan. I realized New York City was open to the kind of architecture I wanted to explore. My attraction to the city was so strong that I never left. After 35 years of practice, I still get excited by opportunities and challenges that present themselves every day. Even within somewhat rigid rules— zoning, codes, budgets—there is so much that can be done. It's like working on a large puzzle and getting the pieces to fit together in both scale and aesthetics.

I started my own architectural practice in 1972, earning commissions for residential, school and daycare projects in the metropolitan area. Media coverage helped put my practice on the map—first there was coverage of the conversion of a single family home on Long Island to a nursery school; later the media noted a project in which I converted a decommissioned army barracks to a Montessori school in New Jersey. The attention led to more school and parks projects. I was enjoying myself, and even started a company called "Environments for Children" that offered a "kit-of-parts" for play spaces in daycare centers, schools and parks. This "kit-of-parts," naturally, evolved from my work designing children's play environments.

The late 1970s brought about a new administration policy in Washington, D.C., and unfortunately funding for children's daycare facilities all but disappeared. I was forced to refocus my practice. At the same time, in a major push to gentrify marginal neighborhoods, New York City began offering economic tax incentives. Thus, I decided to become an architect/developer for small to mid-size, luxury urban housing. Key to my decision was that it put me in a position to produce buildings that, as an architect, I wanted to design—without having to compromise my objectives. I was also lured by the challenge to achieve and maintain high-quality design in a speculative market place.

As architect/developer, I began an in-depth exploration of many areas, including the impact of building codes and zoning resolutions and how they give direction to the design process; the manipulation of light and space; the fabric of a neighborhood and its impact on private living environments; and how to pursue attainable, cost-effective solutions while meeting a project's functional, budgetary and aesthetic objectives. I always deal with the reality of the budget no matter how minimal. My approach is rarely one of subtraction/deletion from what I design. Instead, I believe it's both more responsible and more efficient to be in a position to add to the building design in the event the client is able to support more. Creating special experiences that are visually surprising and dramatic doesn't have to cost more money; in fact, they can become invaluable marketing tools if pursued creatively.

Someone once told me, "You have the mind of an investment banker and the soul of a poet." Well, the process of putting "the deal" together has always been—and still is—an exciting part of every project. It's particularly exhilarating to evaluate a site's potential faster than a competitor who might bring in a whole team to do an analysis. As a developer, I selected prominent sites, thus challenging myself as an architect to design better buildings. Prominent sites also helped attract investors for new projects. As an architect competing in an active housing market, I started with a simple palette of materials typical to speculative housing in New York City. The key was putting the materials together in powerful yet comfortable ways. This approach put me on a level playing field with other developers; that is, the cost of materials didn't price me out of the market place, and it lessened the possibility of having to sacrifice or compromise on design.

In the late 1980s, the economy crashed. Never would I have predicted that my vision for combining straightforward materials and realistic budgets with a strong design aesthetic would serve me so well. Indeed, institutional financing of luxury and market-rate housing came to an abrupt halt. Ironically, money was newly available for New York City- and state-funded projects, the majority of which were in the outer New York City boroughs of the Bronx, Brooklyn, Queens and Staten Island. Instead of luxury and market-rate apartment buildings in Manhattan, there was a call for transitional and permanent housing facilities for people who were homeless, mentally ill and living with AIDS—basically, no- and low-income housing.

This proved to be an exciting time in my career. I view New York City housing as the most varied, exciting building type there is, and I was committed to becoming an expert. My growing business skills fostered my work as an architect, and I was able to show that quality, thoughtful design could be brought to a New York building sector sadly lacking attention.

For many, supportive housing conjures up horrible images. Yet I found that the architectural issues in these project types were essentially the same ones I faced when designing luxury and market-rate housing. I decided to hang up my hat as a Manhattan developer and instead provide architectural services to nonprofit housing organizations. Instead of working in upscale midtown Manhattan, I took my design philosophy of simple materials, realistic budgets, and "stretching-the-envelope" design into deteriorated sections of the Bronx, Brooklyn and Queens. After some adjustment, I realized that my design philosophy did not have to change. Only the location of my projects changed. Here was a chance to create quality architecture in areas not accustomed to much environmental attention. The need for supportive and low-income housing was enormous, and I could make a difference. It was important for me to bring these buildings to an architectural level not previously seen. I am proud to have helped change the landscape of urban low-income and nonprofit housing.

My relationships and experiences in both the luxury and low-income markets prepared me well for the new millennium, which I believe will combine both luxury and affordable housing. With the economy in full swing since 1996, luxury residential development in New York City (in Manhattan and in the boroughs) has flourished and, in turn, fueled a significant amount of affordable housing development. Both are areas of continuing activity, and ones that I enjoy working in, with challenges that are exciting and unending. Today I am doing it all—designing for an array of project types. It all comes down to experience and the ability to participate in the public/private partnerships that are instrumental in providing housing for a wide spectrum of New Yorkers.

As an urban architect, I am responsible for designing buildings that stand out—within the context of a neighborhood, keeping in mind that the context will likely change. My work is a collaboration with the future: I create something enduring that other architects will be able to work with as New York City grows.

I happened to be just a few blocks from the World Trade Center when it was attacked and destroyed. This unprecedented, horrible moment in history pushed me, like many people, into a prolonged period of soul searching. I have emerged from that process with my architectural vision intact. Rather than shaking my values, the tragedy has led me to reaffirm my commitment to the creation of quality architecture for the people of New York City.

Still unparalleled in its vibrancy and activity, New York's greatest challenge remains accommodating – both physically and in spirit – the people that crowd into it from the world over. In a place such as this, the creation of housing that serves both the physical needs of its residents, and the architectural needs of its neighborhoods, is one of the most rewarding tasks a person can undertake.

Interpretation is Innovation
by Carlo Paganelli

Architecture whose vocabulary is hard to understand often has something to hide, that ought to be investigated more closely. Perhaps there is a danger of tripping over a sort of "aesthetics of real estate profits" if we run away from our architectural responsibilities. This certainly is not the case with Meltzer, because his experimentation works along the systematic lines of carefully gauged design and elegant use of materials. Of course, this has nothing to do with a symphony of forms. His architecture is a far cry from the rather outmoded poetics of architecture as so-called "frozen music". Meltzer is also poles apart from those whose fear of exposing themselves too much leads to a sort of cancelling out of all new ideas, inevitably falling into the trap of blandness. In Meltzer's work, there is a real awareness of a cityscape like New York, whose endless array of cultural-artistic opportunities shape and re-shape the urban environment, inevitably exercising a notable influence on the co-ordinates of architectural design. Meltzer is a careful observer of New York in its entirety, not just the dazzlingly spectacular architecture of Manhattan, but also of the Bronx, Staten Island, Queens, and Harlem. This underlines the idea that architecture is, above all, a public practice and not a three-dimensional autobiography of the latest designer to break into the mainstream.

One particular building is most emblematic of this design philosophy: the Crotona Avenue Apartments. This block of over eighty apartments shows how architecture out in the real world is not just the occasional "eye-catcher" by the stars of design, but first and foremost practical constructions in which the creator's contribution never breaks the rules of zoning, financial investments, the clients' wishes, or even the socio-cultural extraction of the people destined to live in the buildings. In other words, Meltzer treats architecture more as interpretation than stylistic innovation. It might be added that the art of building is not just a solid, concrete narrative of events spread across time and history, it also has a soul in harmony with the global order it fits into. This can only be achieved by drawing on an easily understandable language of forms.

The concept informing Meltzer's architecture is connected to noble fathers of American architecture like Jefferson, who dedicated himself, heart and soul, to observing the order of nature and who drew on the basic principles of art to interpret the age and place in which he lived and worked. Meltzer tends to interpret the guidelines of tradition in a modern key. He has absolutely no intention of reinventing architecture from scratch. On the contrary, each of his works is intended to show how each act of design, as regards both its urban form and architectural content, is the product of a constant, complex process of sedimentation and is, above all, a conscientious act. Architectural progress cannot ignore what is already there, or in other words the forms and contents of architecture do not lose their meaning when they are transferred into different historical settings. Of course, we need to decide what still reflects certain cultural values and what never loses its aesthetic worth, and discard what is really nothing more than sheer mannerism. The important thing is to respect the evolutionary dynamics of architecture without forcing the controls of individual creativity. In this sense, Meltzer's work is even more clearly outlined by a quote like: "Modernity: an unfinished project", which was the title of a famous architectural exhibition held in Paris in the early-1980s.

Incompleteness is actually the ideal way to describe the permanent state of contemporary architecture, taken as a synthesis of a dynamic ideology and constantly changing society.

Taking the Crotona Avenue Apartments as a startling example of Meltzer's work, due to the way it perfectly reflects its urban surroundings, we can see how meaningful architecture can be built without resorting to postmodernist/historicist citation or exasperatingly high-tech exercises in style. This means neither bending to the classical-academic dogmas of the Greek temple nor focusing on technological details such as, for instance, structural glass, as the distinctive feature of a building's identity. The same goes for just letting computer technology take its own course, as the latest generation of the sophisticated CAD program is set to work on complex spatial configurations that look like amoebas floating in cyberspace. Computers are now an inevitable part of the design process, but we must not forget they are just tools, and not the art directors of architectural firms.

As regards modernity and its implications for design, it is interesting to note how Meltzer relates to his own era. Somebody once described the contemporary age as the "second machine age", or in other words the electronics or telematics age. From the point of view of design, Meltzer seems to conform to the man-machine or nature-artifice antinomy, giving precedence to the sculptural nature of forms rather than technological components, side-stepping issues of little interest like examining a building's rationalist, brutalist, expressionist or organic matrixes, etc., now that debate between critics, architects and clients has shifted away from these rather obvious categories.

The traditional canons of criticism are now totally obsolete. It is taken for granted that all buildings are functional since they are built according to building regulations corresponding to specific structural constraints. The project's distinctive so-called "ideological" features are evident in the more or less visible way the architect fits in with modern-day society and in the work's most positive values.

Nowadays, for instance, careful attention is paid to a building's communicative force, which has broken down the critical unity of architecture and brought out the specific, unique values of four-dimensional space in contrast to traditional works of architecture. Semiological studies into architecture have produced effects with wide-reaching ramifications, including the abandonment of the idea of analysing architecture along solely formal/aesthetic lines.

Total aperture is now one of the key concepts in reading contemporary architecture. American architecture shows that the pluralistic fragmentation of architectural styles does not prevent developments in stylistic idioms. Whereas in the past architecture gave visual form to a certain ethnic dominion, it now tends to designate islands of meaning. In Meltzer's case, for instance, the road becomes an archetype of space. It reflects the general tendency of homo viator. American cities were built up around their streets, with their grid layouts suggesting the idea of equal opportunities in all choices.

Fundamental aspect of Meltzer's designs is the typological side of his buildings. This evokes the idea of instantly recognising the practical function of a work of architecture. This means every building will have its own figurative quality related to its oldest archetype. In this respect Meltzer is an architect deeply grounded in American tradition.

The bonds between Meltzer's work and American architectural tradition emerge in certain fundamental archetypes of urban architecture like the congregational building. Melrose Court in the Bronx draws on aspects of the earliest community buildings by working with simple structures with no ornamentation or elaborate stylistic features. The stylistic essence of the building is instantly communicated: the basic volume immediately evokes its practical purpose. Secondly, the simplicity of its forms reveals its spatial layout, corresponding not only to function but also to the idea of the actions and orientation of an individual. In the case of a congregational building, these aspects provide a certain idea of man and his place in the world, that lies at the very foundations of American civilisation.

The American civilisation has produced skyscrapers, an icon condensing the spirit of modernity. The skyscraper is not a very regular part of Meltzer's work, which tends to focus more on styles designed to project corporate images. For Meltzer, not particularly involved in post-modern architecture, it is quite significant that his design for the Queens West Development Project, in New York, is supposed to be a heart-felt tribute to Philip Johnson, one of the greatest post-modernist masters. Meltzer took a complex constructed around mainly rigidly orthogonal forms and inserted his own personal rendering of the famous building at 53rd Street and Third Avenue in Manhattan, known as "the lipstick building" due to its distinctive, elegant form.

Even though citation, or homage if you like, is a common practice in all the arts and can be found right down the ages, it is worth taking a special look at its role in architecture. The fact that a building is a constantly visible, public object requiring the investment of capital means that those involved in its construction deserve some sort of openly flaunted, overt credit. Particularly if the citation in question concerns a building in their own city. Needless to say, nobody can patent a geometric form for this purpose, in this case the ellipse characterising the horizontal section of both Lipstick and the tower complex designed by Meltzer. Here, in particular, Meltzer was interested in reflecting on the idea of interpreting architecture in terms of its mirroring force. After all, if architecture really is an unfinished project, then it ought to contain fragments of other works of architecture and design.

Traces and signs, drawn from both near and far, are important aspects of the work of a very American architect like Meltzer. The skyscraper is an unavoidable model and, most significantly, key symbol of power in American culture. If we work on the assumption that churches symbolise religious power and castles stand for the aristocratic ruling class, then skyscrapers are the architectural embodiment of multi-national companies. These great cathedrals of trade are capable of representing certain significant aspects of the economic forces governing the age in which we live. They are perhaps the ultimate in height, form and effect. In a deliberate attempt to strike the public's imagination, we have managed to design structures so loaded with messages that they actually interfere with the skyline of modern-day cities. It almost seems as if image has reached the highest possible degree of self-reference now that it has nothing left to measure itself up to. But there has also been a certain inversion in this trend as the skyscraper's content and image are gradually being stitched back together. Architectural design is inevitably the product of a generative process drawing on a system of logical and also creative rules to give a definite structure to a certain portion of matter. This seems to be so obvious that it is almost a platitude. But it is worth remembering that the post-modern movement managed to make its presence felt for years while completely ignoring all this.

Experimentation is now moving in other directions as new and complex problems are beginning to emerge on the world architectural scene. We must be very careful to ensure that architecture is still treated as a public affair and not left in the hands of just a few leading lights of its star system. The rapidly spreading phenomenon of the so-called communication city must be knit into the urban environment and not be the only vital presence in the midst of the relics of our ancient cities. Media culture weaves the products of industrial civilisation, like machines, paths, flyovers, railways etc., into a web of icons and texts run by systems like the Internet, as well as the film industry, television, and newspapers. Our vision of the material city is tending more and more to be replaced by a non-material city and the new rules that govern it. All this tends to accelerate change. The city was beginning to look as if it had been buried beneath a random, chaotic patchwork of architecture with no definite identity. The new cityscape looks like a boundless territory composed of thousands of other cities spread across the globe and connected together in cyberspace by telecommunications networks and by the people using these icons, services, and transport systems etc.

In other words, the modernist city really seems to be on the road to change. Pathways of buildings, places of worship, and squares are no longer so indispensable thanks to the development of media highways. The telecommunications network ignores the material side of the city as it develops its own ideal space. So what is the architect's role in a scenario in which the very material of building is dissolving? Among the various paths opening up recently, there is a definite trend towards protecting the environment, safeguarding the city's historical sites, and using new technology for services, the control of migratory flows, and culture. The living city strategically injects value into what are now its most fundamental places: craft quarters, areas full of monuments, landscaping, and cutting-edge technology. But Las Vegas must not provide the only urban guidelines on planet Earth. So what can we do about all this? One answer might be to create rules capable of blocking the daily flow of minor changes that tend to alter and destructure the city's image. In the end, we basically need to design projects protecting the grounding identity of western cities. Meltzer's work, with its inherent awareness of the city scape, can lead the way.

Works

Development Projects

Architects are frequently asked to describe how they approach a given project. For many, the answers vary from project to project. For Meltzer, there is a single most influential factor contributing to how he now approaches a project: the experience of designing and developing his own projects. During the 1980s, he had the opportunity to be both architect and developer. "I acquired first-hand knowledge of what a client looks for in an architect" Meltzer says, "and began to understand what role the architect plays for the client. I learned that, in many instances, architects are not necessarily sensitive to, or understanding of, a client's issues, particularly when the client is a real estate developer. By expanding my frame of reference, becoming more flexible, and intently listening, I could ultimately satisfy a developer's needs without compromising my architectural goals."

Another question posed frequently to architects is "What is the definition of a successful project?" A successful project is not the result of quality architecture alone; it is the result of quality architecture completed on time and within the parameters of a defined budget. "In my experience as architect and developer, the budgets were indeed defined, and every day of delay affected our return on investment, negatively. This practical experience—everything from the difficulties and crises, especially in the construction phase, to the successes—made me appreciate the delicate balance of a successful project. And most important, I gained a solid foundation of practical knowledge that I draw on every day in my professional life. In fact, the frustration of architect-client-contractor relationships moved me to create my own construction entity, BDL Construction Corporation."

Marvin H. Meltzer Architects begin the architect-developer series by looking at a modest rehab of an existing building—a property that changed dramatically despite a minimal budget. With each successive project, gradually the size and scope of the buildings increased. The last in the series of architect-developer projects, a new, 22-story mixed-use building, topped-off my development career. Alas, because of the decline in the economy, the project was never built.

"As you will see in the projects represented," Meltzer says, "I was challenged by the goal of doing more with less. I surveyed the materials that other residential developers in the city were using, and eventually my design philosophy emerged: use the same materials but deliver a better product.

I was determined to assemble the materials in the most compelling, exciting way possible. I felt deep gratification when the public and media received the projects with enthusiasm."

There are some constant themes that developed during these projects that flow through to his work today. Meltzer has always felt that bringing some outdoor space into a project, where possible, enhances it enormously. Perhaps he was influenced by his upbringing in a less dense urban environment where outdoor space was viewed differently; or perhaps he was motivated by New York City's lack of outdoor space. In any event, very early on, the use of courtyards as transitional spaces became a key element, or theme, of his work. Another theme has been the creation of interior spaces that borrow from each other and bring natural light to the interior of the building. These elements are most rare in the New York City environment.

Hudson Street Townhouses
New York, NY

Completion Date
1982

Owner/Developer
Britton Development, Ltd.

Architects
Marvin H. Meltzer Architects, P.C.

Principal Architect
Marvin H. Meltzer, AIA, NCARB

Consultants
Structural Engineer
Marvin H. Meltzer Architects, P.C.
Mechanical Engineer
Marvin H. Meltzer Architects, P.C.

Construction
BDL Construction

Photography
Dan Cornish

TECHNICAL DATA

Square Footage
3,814

Number of Stories
4

Number of Units
2

Framing System
Masonry bearing walls; wood joists.

Exterior Finishes
Brick and stucco.

Exterior Waterproofing
Built up roofing.

H.V.A.C.
Hot water baseboard radiators; gas fired boiler and domestic hot water.

Interior Partitions
Painted gypsum board drywall and wood base.

Residential Interior Finishes
Hollow metal door frames and wood doors. Skim coat plaster ceiling, marble tile floors and tub surroundings. Wood floor kitchens with granite counter tops.

Security and Fire Protection
Ceiling mounted smoke detectors in units.

Located in the historic Greenwich Village neighborhood of Manhattan, 449 (and later 449 $^1/_2$) Hudson Street was a vacant, three-story, 25-foot-wide nondescript warehouse building waiting for an innovative solution. The goal was to create two side-by-side homes that would maximize the investment potential and at the same time deliver comfortable unique living spaces.

Architecturally, this site was attractive because it offered an opportunity to create a dynamic tension between old (the façade) and new (the interior). While the brick and shuttered façade was researched and fully restored to its original character, under the guidance of the Landmark Preservation Commission, the interior was completely redesigned and constructed as two contemporary homes, each 12 feet wide. This approach proved to have a major impact on several future projects—most significantly, Melrose Court in the South Bronx where 12-foot-wide units were again designed.

In New York City, the average New Yorker usually has an option of either quality of space or quantity of space. My architectural goal for the Hudson Street Townhouses was to offer both. Rarely do rooms in New York City apartments exceed 12-foot-wide dimensions, so the width of each house and the proportion of the spaces posed no real problems. The challenge was how to create vertical circulation through the house and still maintain appropriate living areas. The solution was to create an open stair in the middle of the house, thus allowing comfortable, well proportioned living spaces in the front and back of the building.

The interior combines dramatic lighting, glass block, exposed brick walls and polished oak floors. The units have fireplaces in the living room, dining room and master bedroom. The living room has a service kitchen. The master bedroom suite occupies the entire second floor, with the sleeping area in the quiet rear of the property. Two more bedrooms occupy the top floor. The dining room is at the lowest level, where the boiler room used to be. There are two and a half baths in each unit. Sliding glass doors off the living room open onto a terrace in the rear yard, which is also accessible to the lower level dining room. The two homes capture pieces of the past, as reflected in the restoration of original fireplaces and exposed brick walls, and are naturally integrated into the important historic character of Greenwich Village.

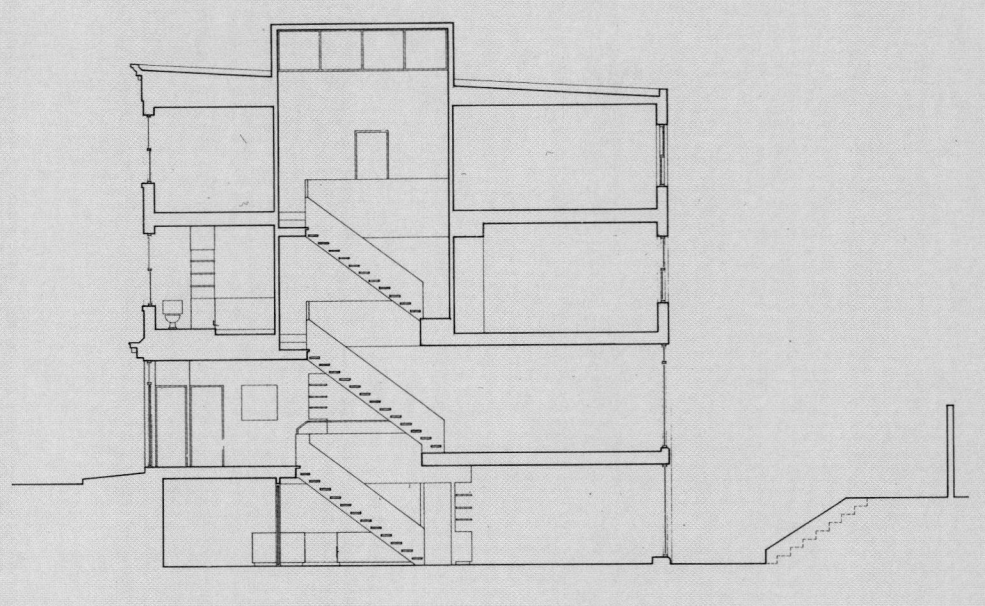

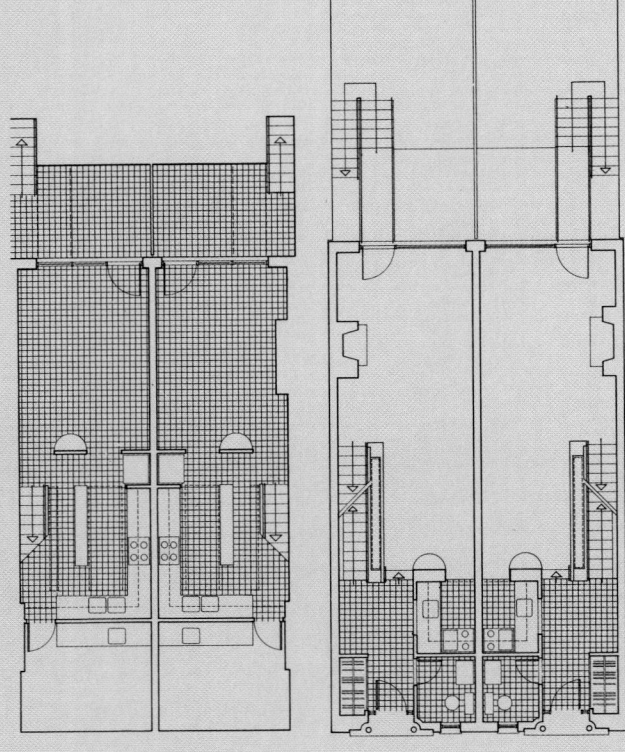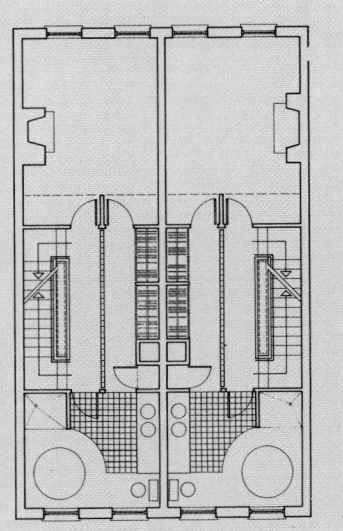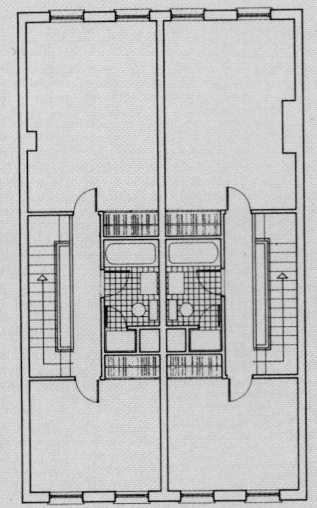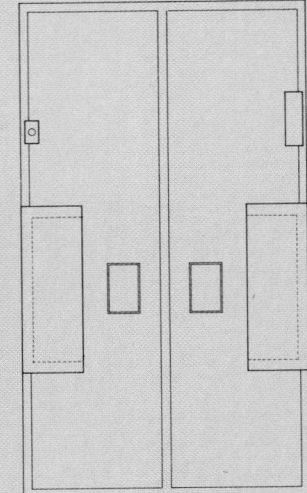

Top, cross section looking south.

Above from left, lower/dining room level plan, entrance/living room level plan, master bedroom suite plan, upper level/bedrooms plan, roof plan.

Right, axonometric view.

Caption.

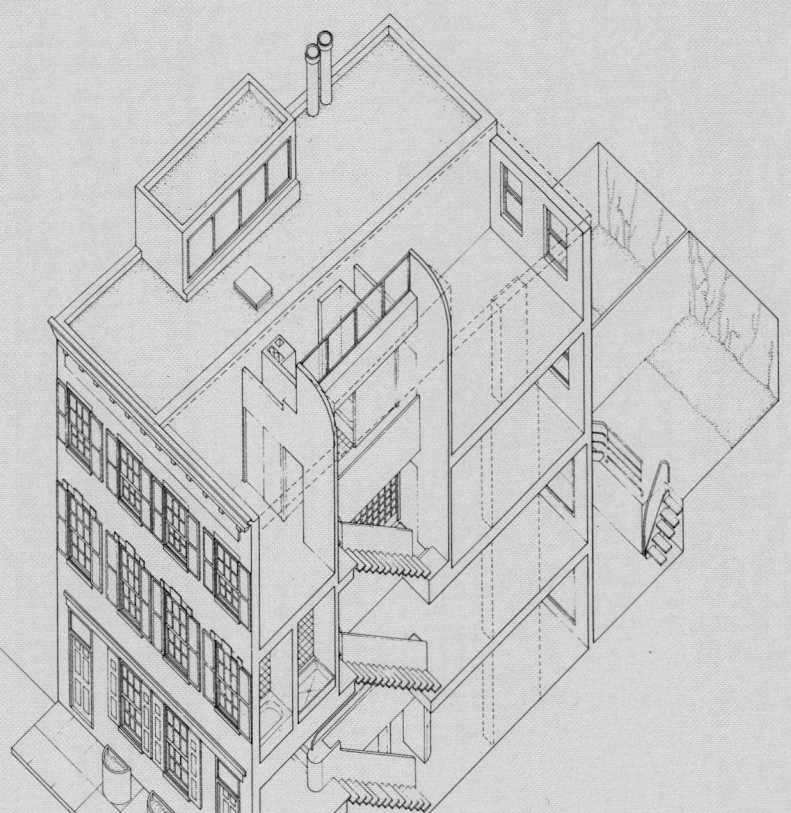

Top left, view of living room looking toward the townhouse entry.

Top right, balcony at fourth floor showing clerestory light into the stairwell.

Above, master-bedroom suite looking into dressing area and master bath.

Left, living room from the entry and view to dining room downstairs.

100 West 81st Street
New York, NY

Date
1983

Owner/Developer
Britton Devlopment, Ltd.

Architects
Marvin H. Meltzer Architects, P.C.

Principal Architect
Marvin H. Meltzer, AIA, NCARB

Project Managers
Steven Conners-Residential

David Abelow-Restaurant

Consultants
Structural Engineer
Anthony Vairamides
Mechanical Engineer
Emil Grunberg, P.E.

Photography
Danon's on the Park
Dan Cornish

TECHNICAL DATA

Square Footage
23,830 total square footage
4,700 – restaurant
19,130 - residential

Number of Stories
7

Number of Units
16

Framing System
Masonry bearing-wall, wood joist framing, steel girders.

Exterior Finishes
Brick and stucco.

Exterior Waterproofing
Built-up roofing with wood deck.

Vertical Transportation
Hydraulic elevators.

H.V.A.C.
Thru-wall air conditioning units, individually controlled fin tube radiators, central gas fired boiler and domestic hot water.

Interior Partitions
Painted gypsum board drywall and wood base.

Residential Interior Finishes
Wood strip flooring, painted gypsum board drywall, ceramic tile kitchen and bathroom, exposed brick.

Public Corridor Finishes
Carpet, gypsum board walls and ceilings.

Residential Lobby Finishes
Slate, gypsum board, glass block.

Security and Fire Protection
Line voltage smoke detectors.

At the time of this rehab, the southwest corner of Columbus Avenue and West 81st Street was the far-reaching fringe of Manhattan's trendy Upper West Side. For the forward-thinking developer, however, the location seemed destined for improvement. The fact that the property sits directly across the street from the American Museum of Natural History and enjoys unobstructed views of Central Park were unique circumstances that played a role in how the project developed.

Four contiguous four-story row houses, dating from around 1920, had been left empty for years. A previous developer, intending to create 30 rental units on the assembled lot, failed to get the project off the ground. The architect's successful track record with several rehab development projects suggested that this project could also be a success. The approach was to unify the buildings and create a variety of loft spaces to be sold as co-ops to the upwardly mobile. Adding two-and-a-half floors to the tenement buildings allowed for a total of 16 co-op loft units, half of them duplexes, ranging in size from 870 to 1,633 square feet. The ground floor and basement commercial space was ideal for a restaurant.

The addition helped unify the four buildings architecturally. With six stories—the limit for a wood-joist, non-fireproof building in New York City—the building is in keeping with the area's character. As much of the original structure as possible was retained, allowing existing building walls to determine the apartment shapes. Floor elevations —differing by as much as 18 inches to two feet — were left as they were, connected by stairs either in the apartments or in hallways. Original window openings and stone lintels above them were preserved, while some windows were enlarged and new corner glazing added. The only structural change was the addition of new columns to reinforce spans throughout the building and at the corners. A new elevator and public stairways were added at the rear of the site. Problems in finding matches for the old brick size and color meant that the buildings had to be painted, an element that tied the addition to the existing buildings. The sculpted stucco fire balconies, a New York City code requirement, also help coordinate the two parts. This was the firm's third attempt at combining brick and stucco — it has gradually evolved into a key aspect of its current work and is reflected most strongly in my current low-income projects.

The units feature oak floors, terraces, corner windows, high ceilings and 12-inch masonry walls, exposed where practical. The top-floor apartments are duplexes with roof terraces—finished with wood decking plus balconies—and spiral staircases in the units. The interior finishes and partitions, except for four units designed as models, were left unfinished to give buyers the most flexibility in planning. One of the finished units, the corner penthouse, features walls disengaged from the ceiling to allow the maximum penetration of natural light. The double height space and clerestory are engaged by an interior façade with a curved window penetration suitable for a child's bedroom which affords a view of Central Park. The curve reflects an important planter/storage area at the first floor.

Finally, the project included converting the four existing ground floor commercial spaces and rear yard area into one 130-seat restaurant. The four existing spaces and a new green house enclosure form a cohesive whole, yet are identifiable as individual rooms. Dropped ceilings, alluding to canopied outdoor cafes, create natural areas for seating groups. Glazing in relation to the street and yard further invoke this impression.

This project was an extremely rewarding experience, possibly the firm's most exciting design of all. Meltzer acted as developer, architect and contractor, designing the penthouse apartment and four other apartments in the building, as well as the restaurant.

Right, from bottom up: first floor showing plan of restaurant and apartment building lobby, second floor showing model apartment, fourth and fifth floors showing typical flats and duplex layouts.

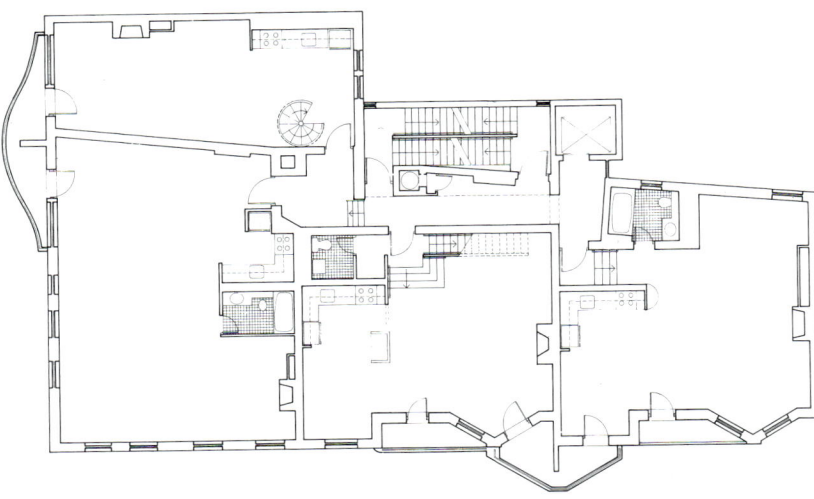

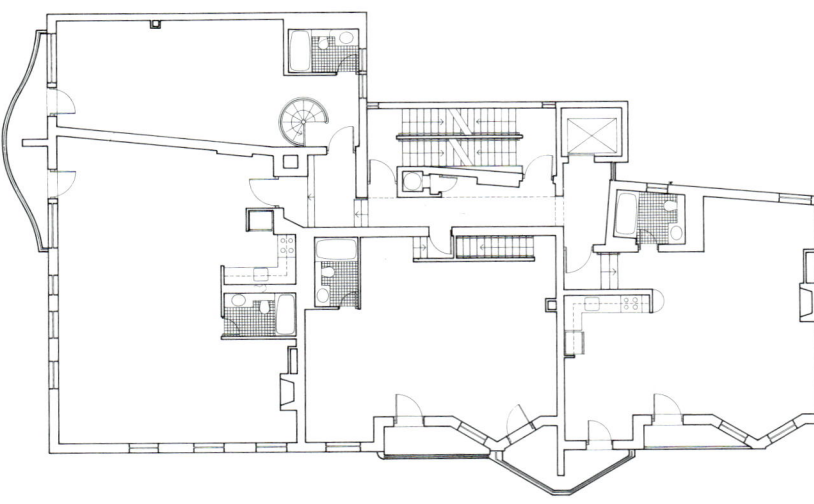

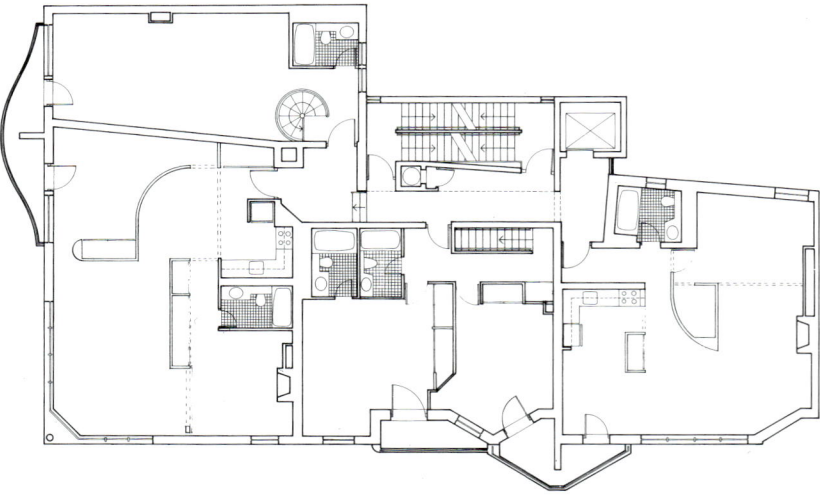

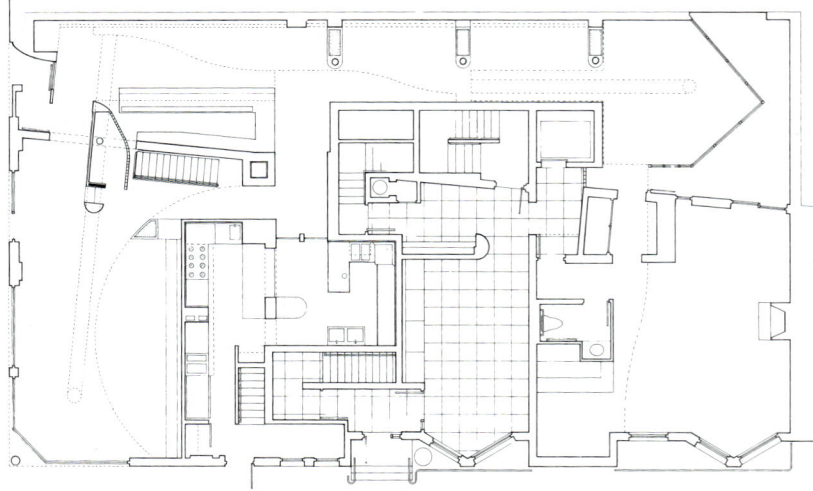

Above, view looking up at fire balconies on West 81st Street. These were code requirements for egress that were used as architectural elements.

Above left, view of penthouse living room looking toward kitchen. The curved windows in the two-story space are in the child's bedroom to allow a view of Central Park.

Above right, view looking out to exterior roof deck with a view of Central Park and the Museum of Natural History.

Above, view from fifth floor apartment looking toward Central Park. The sliding Shoji screen was used to define the den space.

Left, restaurant, looking toward bar area and coatroom.

Below, restaurant main dining room with curved form above seating area acting as a canopy and the mirrored wall reflecting the street activity outside.

Greencroft Condominiums
New Rochelle, NY

Completion Date
1984

Owner/Developer
Horst Vollman

Development Consultant
Marvin H. Meltzer, AIA, NCARB

Architects
Marvin H. Meltzer Architects, P.C.

Principal Architect
Marvin H. Meltzer, AIA, NCARB

Project Architect
James Crisp

Consultants Structural Engineer
Berkenfeld-Getz Associates
Great Neck, NY

Mechanical Engineer
Toder/Schwartz

Landscape Architect
William B. Kuhl

Photography
Steven Fischer

TECHNICAL DATA

Square Footage
112,356

Number of Stories
6 stories plus parking

Number of Units
148

Framing System
Masonry bearing walls, precast concrete floor plank.

Exterior Finishes
Steel stud panels faced with 8" by 8" quarry tile and European ceramic tile, split faced concrete block.

Exterior Waterproofing
Built up roofing system.

Vertical Transportation
Hydraulic elevators.

H.V.A.C.
Individually controlled fan coin units, central oil fired boilers and domestic hot water.

Interior Partitions
Two (2) hour fire rated gypsum drywall, 50 STC between apartment units.

Residential Interior Finishes
Hardwood floors, painted gypsum board drywall, hollow metal door frames, wood doors, kadex ceiling treatment, ceramic tile kitchen floors and bathroom floors and tub surrounds.

Public Corridor Finishes
Carpet, vinyl wall covering, incandescent accent light, slate saddle and wall base. All materials class "A" flame spread.

Residential Lobby Finishes
Pink Salisbury granite flooring, natural wood trim, custom light fixtures.

Security and Fire Protection
Monitored gateway entrance, doorman.

Within a 20-minute drive of New York City is the town of New Rochelle. In this Westchester County suburb, apartment buyers of multifamily housing had only two options: duplex townhouses or multi-story apartment buildings. Greencroft Condominium was completed in 1984 to offer a more contemporary approach to the suburban market: a luxury mid-rise condominium complex. Tenants desired the so-called good life of the suburbs, the elegance of a traditional home and the ease, service and comfort of condominium living.

Greencroft Condominium—a 148-unit development on 3.4 acres—sits adjacent to the Pelham Country Club to the south and overlooks Long Island Sound. The two six-story buildings designed, only one of which was built, are situated on a 70-foot-high slope offering views of the country club's verdant golf course on one side and the soothing water of the Long Island Sound on the other. The masonry bearing wall, precast concrete plank structure carries prefabricated lightweight panels faced with European ceramic tile that enclose the building. The 21' x 8'8-high panels were manufactured in Pennsylvania, shipped to the site, hoisted by crane into place and welded to angles set in the plank. Windows, railings, incremental units and skylights were then installed in the field. Proximity to the water influenced the choice of colors for the front and rear tile panel elevations: tones of grey, cream, black and green accented by blue-green railings. The exterior masonry blocks on the base and side walls are finished to evoke rock-faced granite.

Greencroft Condominium was the architect's first experience with masonry bearing wall, concrete plank structural systems. The system proved to be very cost effective, but rigid and unforgiving in attempts to provide form or expression to the building. This was the beginning of his treating flat facades as canvases for color compositions.

The underlying philosophy is that people seek to live in places that uniquely express their individuality. Greencroft Condominium includes 82 one-bedroom apartments and 66 two-bedroom apartments, with 13 apartments per floor, ranging in size from 900 to 1,800 square feet. Nine penthouse apartments in each building feature continuous skylights with reflective bronze glazing extending over the bedroom, living room and exposed terrace.

Landscaping brings a central focus to the site. A rock garden separates the levels of the two buildings, and organizes parking and interior circulation. The development contains outdoor parking for 98 cars, indoor space for 120 cars, a tennis court, an outdoor pool and fitness and spa facilities.

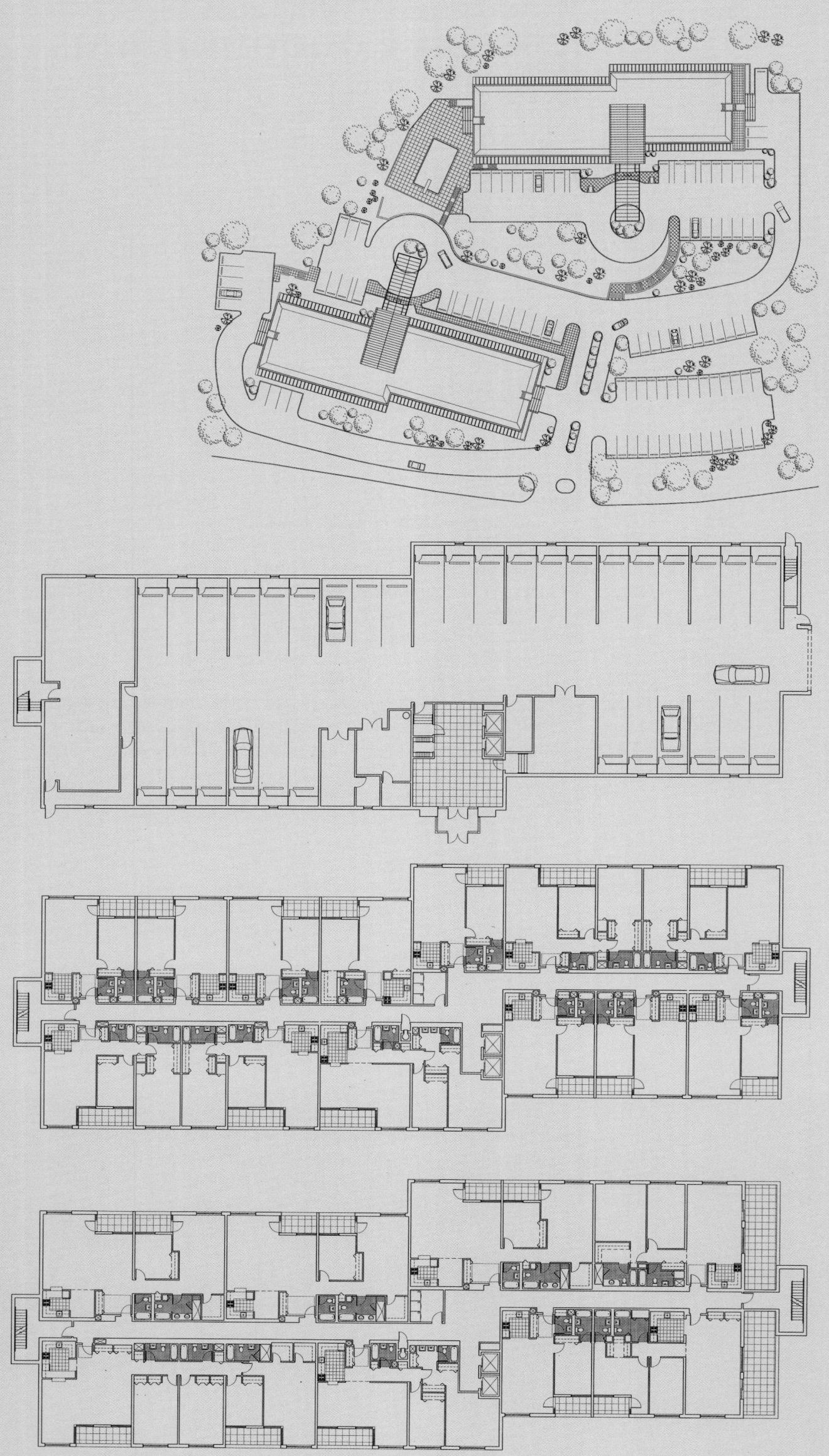

Left from top,
site plan showing two
proposed buildings,
parking garage level,
typical floor,
penthouse floor.

Top left, view of entry and front façade from on-site tennis court.

Top right, view of front façade from entry drive showing split face block at parking garage level and pre-fabricated ceramic tile panels above.

Above, view of façade facing golf course with pre-fabricated ceramic tile panels and a continuous skylight at the penthouse level.

The Enclave
New York, NY

Completion Date
1986

Owner/Developer
Britton Development, Ltd.

Architects
Marvin H. Meltzer Architects, P.C.

Principal Architect
Marvin H. Meltzer, AIA, NCARB

Project Manager
Angelo Rodriguez

Consultants
Structural Engineer
Antony Vairamides, P.E.

Mechanical Engineer
George Langer, P.E.

Photography
Mark C. Darley
Steven Fischer

TECHNICAL DATA

Square Footage
40,000

Number of Stories
16

Number of Units
25

Framing System
Cast in place reinforced concrete columns and flat plate slab.

Exterior Waterproofing
Built-up pre "IRMA" type roofing system with gravel and/or precast stone pavers.

Vertical Transportation
Geared traction automatic elevators.

H.V.A.C.
Individually controlled fan coin units, central oil fired boilers and domestic hot water.

Interior Partitions
Two (2) hour fire rated gypsum drywall, 50 STC between apartment units.

Residential Interior Finishes
Hardwood floors, painted gypsum board drywall, hollow metal door frames, wood doors, kadex ceiling treatment, ceramic tile kitchen floors and bathroom floors and tub surrounds.

Public Corridor Finishes
Carpet, vinyl wall covering, incandescent accent light, slate saddle and wall base. All materials class "A" flame spread.

Residential Lobby Finishes
Slate floors, wood, slate and metal walls, fluorescent cove lighting and incandescent spot lighting.

Security and Fire Protection
Doorman, closed-circuit television and electrically activated door strike at fenced plaza and residential entry vestibule, line voltage smoke detectors in units.

In the development of Manhattan real estate, the term "sliver building" was coined to describe the tall, narrow (and often-criticized) structures that tower over adjacent low-rise town houses or apartment buildings. With an explosion in real estate values in the early 1980s, approximately 30 such buildings were constructed in luxury-district neighborhoods on the East and West Sides. Soon after, the city effectively banned future construction of sliver buildings.

The Enclave is a "sliver" building that breaks the stereotype. It solved a central concern: how to minimize the intrusiveness of a tall, thin structure amid low-rise buildings. The Enclave is a 16-story apartment building, 40 feet wide and 70 feet deep, on a block of largely three-story town houses (faced with brown stone, stucco and limestone) and four- to five-story apartment buildings. The primary goal was to fit the building into the block by minimizing the perception of its height as seen from street level. A second goal was to design a building that echoed the scale and texture of the environment.

The building was given the quality of a brick sculpture, thereby distinguishing it as more than just a tall building. The earthtone brick façade of The Enclave is set back at the eighth and tenth floors, and a pink stucco wall appears to float in front of the façade up at the seventh floor. The pink stucco material softens the building's visual mass and covers the façade most visible from the street. This gesture reflects the texture and scale of the townhouse neighborhood. Fenestration and semicircular balconies further lighten the building's mass. Railings on open balconies visually recall the fire escapes of adjacent apartment buildings.

The 25 condominium apartments in The Enclave offer either northern or southern exposures. Many units on the upper floors have views as far as Queens to the east and to the farthest reaches of the west side of Manhattan. The 12 one-bedroom 900-square-foot units face a park on East 51st Street. Seven two-bedroom apartments of 1,200 square feet and five studio apartments of 665 square feet face 52nd Street. All but one of the studios have balconies or terraces. The 1,500-square-foot duplex apartment at the top of the building has a balcony and 700-square-foot terrace. Apartment layouts were designed individually, floor by floor, with maximum use of natural light, including glass-block walls within the apartments. The interiors feature oak-paneled entry doors, oak floors and window sills, quarry tile kitchen floors, microwave ovens and gas ranges, closed-circuit security system, European-style light switches and stainless steel door levers.

An 8,000-square-foot community facility space on the ground and second floors is designed for medical office suites. The Enclave was Meltzer's first new, flat slab concrete construction project in Manhattan as architect/developer. Overall, it expressed his design philosophy of building luxury apartment buildings with simple, straight-forward materials.

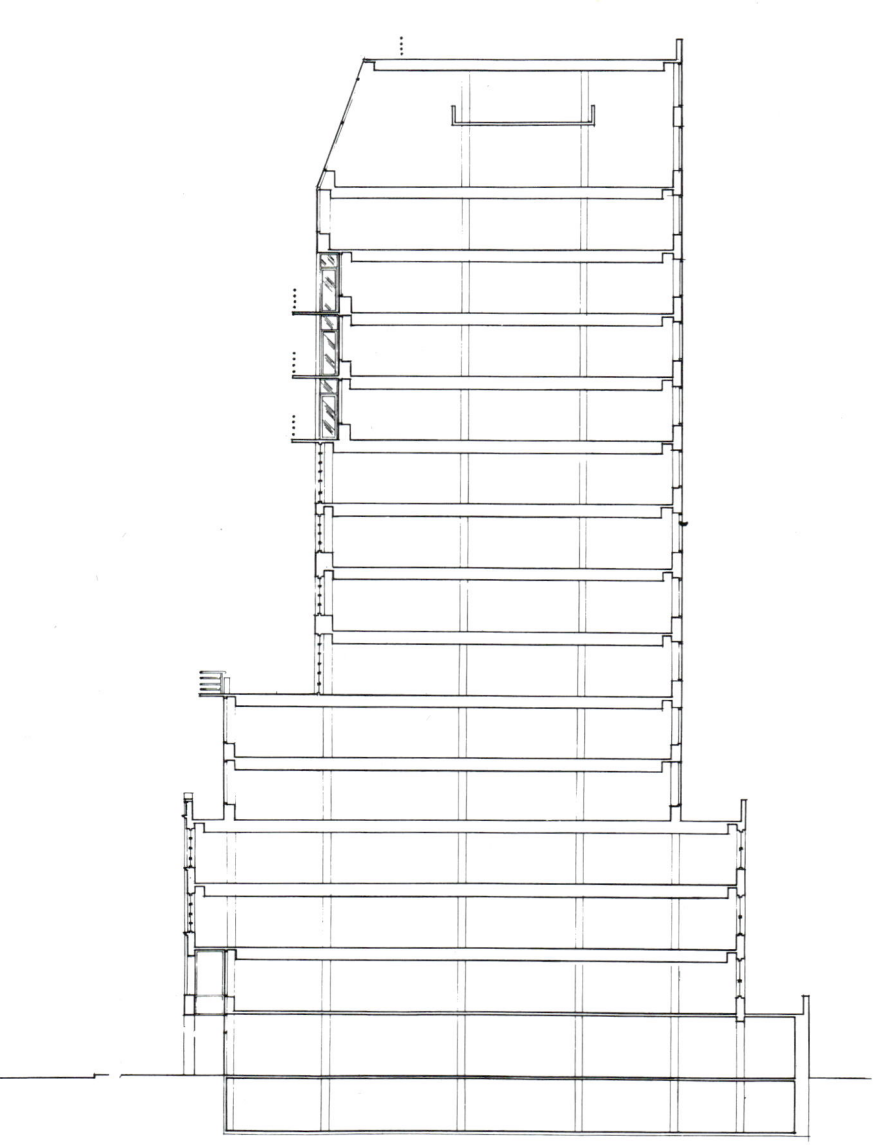

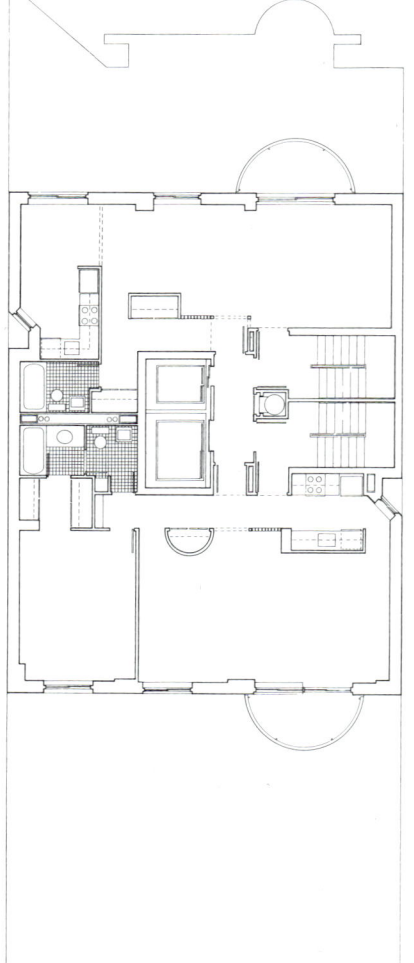

Above, view of building looking north showing balconies and façade articulation. The change in exterior or wall materials reflects the apartments that have a view of Greenacre Park.

Right from top, section, typical floors 2nd-9th, typical floors 10th-14th.

Above from top, view of entrance at night; lobby looking out toward entrance.

Above right, view of pink stucco wall and balconies on front façade that recall the fire escapes of adjoining buildings.

Affordable/Low-Income Housing

The affordable housing projects shown here initially covered the spectrum of no-income or homeless housing and low-income supportive housing, each with a social service component as part of the housing. The people living here include the mentally ill and those suffering from AIDS, as well as senior citizens and battered women. Some projects entailed rehabilitating old buildings; others involved new construction. With every design, adding value was foremost on Meltzer's mind—that is, he wanted to find design solutions that exceeded expectations and went beyond merely typical approaches.

During this period, he worked on a unique site that covered three vacant blocks in the South Bronx. Melrose Court was a public/private partnership project targeted to the for-sale affordable housing market where the population met certain medium-income criteria. He chose an approach that had proven successful in other development and subsidized housing projects. What resulted was beyond even his wildest dreams at the time. The creation of Melrose Court was instrumental in transforming an entire section of the South Bronx. Indeed, Melrose Court's scale, density and massing illustrate how thoughtful, efficient design and simple materials can have a powerful impact. Melrose Court was awarded the Best Affordable Multifamily Housing Project of 1994 by the National Association of Home Builders.

As funding streams changed, Meltzer had several opportunities to design new construction for affordable rental housing projects. Given his history of designing buildings in "less than desirable" neighborhoods, this was a natural evolution for him. The firm built using simple, masonry bearing wall, concrete plank structural systems that are cost effective yet quite rigid and unforgiving. Because such systems are key to the affordability of this housing type, the firm developed a particular vocabulary following a prototype and operating within common limitations. The prototype consists of a percentage of brick and a percentage of Exterior Insulation and Finish System (EIFS). Using this formula, one can explore cost parameters with the client before completing the contract documents. Given the tight time frames around which developers operate, such a prototype can be critical. For example, in one such case, the firm was asked to deliver everything from schematic design through completion of construction in just 16 months. To move that rapidly, the firm had to be thoroughly familiar with all design and construction issues upfront.

A common thread throughout these projects is the use of multi-colored brick and "dryvit" (again, part of a distinct vocabulary Meltzer began using) that create a playful dynamic of form and composition in façade designs. Another common denominator: integrated, comfortable courtyard spaces that are well lit and secure. Since these projects are usually located in rough neighborhoods, attention to such matters can truly affect the overall quality of life for residents. Also, each building design carries a unique identity influenced by the site's location and shape, the zoning regulations and certain funding and agency requirements. Overall, the design clearly enhances the buildings and the surrounding neighborhoods, while adding no further costs to the bottom line.

Melrose Court
Bronx, NY

Completion Date
1994

Owner/Developer
The Procida Organization

Architects
Marvin H. Meltzer Architects, P.C.

Principal Architect
Marvin H. Meltzer, AIA, NCARB

Project Architect
Gloria Glas

Consultants Structural Engineer
Efraim Goldstein

Mechanical Engineer
Toder/Schwartz

Associates Photography
Michael Moran
Paul Warchol

TECHNICAL DATA

Square Footage
261,738

Number of Stories
3- and 4-story buildings

Number of Units
265

Framing System
Masonry bearing wall, precast concrete plank, metal stud exterior walls.

Exterior Finishes
Brick and aluminum siding.

H.V.A.C.
Individually controlled fin tube radiators, central gas fired boiler and domestic hot water.

Interior Partitions
Two hour fire rated gypsum drywall, masonry block between apartments.

Residential Interior Finishes
Carpeting, painted gypsum drywall, hollow metal door-frames with hollow core wood doors, textured paint for ceiling treatment, ceramic tile bathroom floors and tub surroundings, majority of units with awning windows in kitchen.

Public Corridor Finishes
No interior public corridors.

Security and Fire Protection
Line voltage smoke detectors in units.

Melrose Court is an affordable for-sale housing condominium that sits on three city blocks, taking up 4.5 acres, in the South Bronx. This is high-density living (60 units per acre) in a low-rise environment of three and four stories. Each block has a unique design centered on a secure courtyard scheme, and each courtyard is a different shape and size as determined by the street grid. The project contains 265 units and 135 parking spaces. In fact, it was the ability to provide the required parking on the demapped streets that made the density achievable.

The units — two- or three-bedroom apartments for low- and moderate-income families — range from 1,050 square feet to 1,200 square feet. Two building types ultimately determine the mix and the massing.

One is the two-bedroom, floor-through, three-story building; the other, the three-bedroom, floor-through, four-story building. The latter is designed with flats on the lower two levels and two duplex units, side by side, above the flats. The module was such that the width of the flats equaled the width of the two duplexes. The three- and four-story attached buildings resemble townhouses and are situated to provide a safe and secure environment for the residents in a neighborhood that, at the time of development, was not considered safe. Units entered from the street were accessible to handicapped individuals; the other units were entered from the landscaped courtyard.

The architecture is purposefully contradictory in its street and courtyard treatments. The courtyards and their façades are rich and textural, with entrances that recall New York City stoops. Colorful masonry, canopies and a variety of light fixtures all face a landscaped green space with an attractive pattern of walkways and furniture. The street façade, in contrast, takes a minimal approach, using a simple change in the color of the aluminum siding and masonry at the first floor to create interest. The client had, in fact, requested the street facades resemble images of suburban townhouse developments.

The structural system is again masonry bearing wall, concrete plank construction. Unlike other projects that I have designed, the bearing walls are perpendicular to the exterior metal stud walls. The result was eight inches of masonry that eliminated noise between all apartments in the complex—a major consideration in the marketability of the apartments. Melrose Court was a public/private partnership project, and Meltzer worked with a local developer and a nonprofit organization that was supported by local, city, state and federal funds.

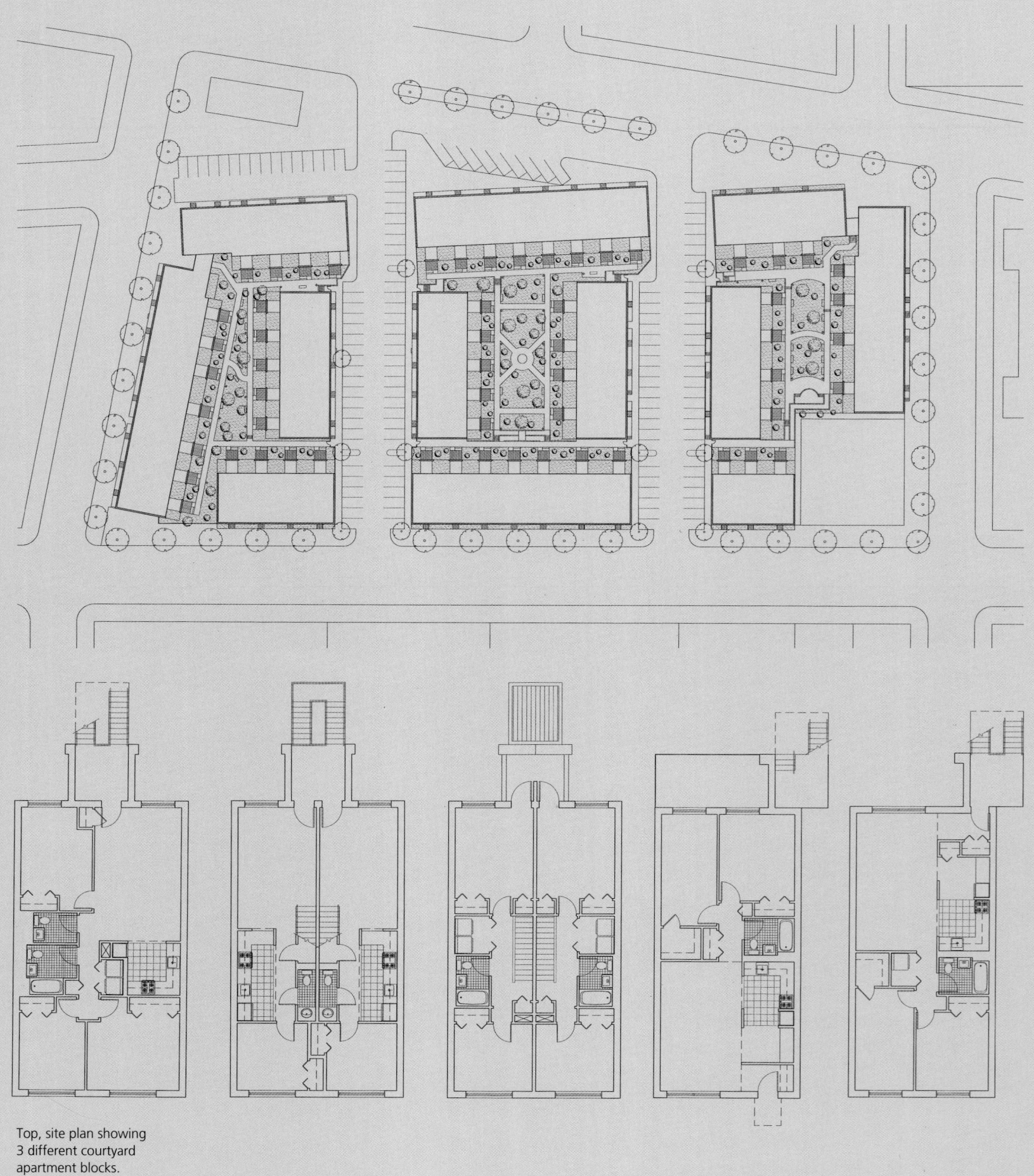

Top, site plan showing 3 different courtyard apartment blocks.

Above from left, typical three-bedroom flat; lower levels of two duplexes - these sit atop the three bedroom flats; upper levels of duplexes; two bedroom handicapped accessible unit; typical two-bedroom flat.

Top, aerial view of entire three block development looking north, showing landscaped courtyards.

Above, looking north at the corner of 157th Street and Brook Avenue.

Top, landscaped interior courtyard of middle block showing precast entrance stairs to all non-handicapped accessible units.

Above, entrance to secure courtyard from parking area.

Right, typical stair entrance from courtyard.

Top, interior of duplex view from kitchen.

Above left, duplex living room view out to balcony.

Above right, duplex living room looking toward kitchen and stair to upper bedroom level.

Carmen B. Bermudez Residence
Bronx, NY

Completion Date
1999

Owner/Developer
Atlantic Deveopment Group, LLC

Architects
Meltzer/Mandl Architects, P.C.

Principal Architect
Marvin H. Meltzer, AIA, NCARB

Project Architect
Dan Heyden

Consultants
Structural Engineer
Robert Silman Associates, P.C.

Mechanical Engineer
John A. DiBari, P.E.

Photography
Elliot Kaufman

TECHNICAL DATA

Square Footage
56,350

Number of Stories
7

Number of Units
72

Framing System
Precast concrete plank, masonry bearing wall, precast concrete lintels.

Exterior Finishes
Three colors of brick, three colors of Exterior Insulation Finishing System (EIFS).

Vertical Transportation
One hydraulic elevator.

H.V.A.C.
Individually controlled fin-tube radiators; central gas fired boiler and domestic hot water.

Interior Partitions
Two hour fire rated gypsum drywall 50 STC between apartments.

Residential Lobby Finishes
Quarry tile flooring with quarry base and paintedd gypsum drywall.

Residential Interior Finishes
VCT flooring, painted gypsum drywall, hollow metal door-frames with hollow core wood doors, textured paint for ceiling treatment, ceramic tile bathroom floors and tub surroundings.

Public Corridor Finishes
Three colors of VCT flooring and vinyl base with painted gypsum drywall and painted CMU, ceiling mounted light fixtures.

Security and Fire Protection
Line voltage smoke detectors in units.

Additional Information
Quality Housing zoning, rear and community room courtyards, elevator lobbies with natural light.

    The Carmen B. Bermudez Residence sits on a deep lot that is 200 ft. deep by 75 ft. wide, unusual in the New York City grid system. Typically, a New York City lot is 100 ft. deep, which allows for a residential building to be suitably wide for double loaded corridors and to provide the 30-foot rear yard mandated by New York City regulations. Also, sites in the Bronx tend to be quite irregular because of the typography and the preponderance of rock in the borough. As such, the depth presented an opportunity to design 36 studios and 36 two-bedroom apartments with a dynamic interior courtyard, while still keeping the building's scale in context with neighboring buildings.

    The landscaped courtyard is unique in ways that contribute to the spirit of the building. It is bounded to the south by a one-story building that houses auto repair shops. This is why it was decided to open up that end of the courtyard to take advantage of an abundance of southern light, as well as to offer wonderful views to the apartment dwellers facing the courtyard. The north wall of the courtyard is designed as a corridor, connecting the building's eastern and western sections. Since the building next door is six stories high and abuts our property, this seemed to be the appropriate location for the connecting corridor. It features an undulating wall highlighted with an abstract, yet unifying, design of three colors of EIFS. Tenants can view the courtyard while moving through the building to and from their apartments.

    The Carmen B. Bermudez Residence was the first of many designed for this client, and it was the first new building built by the client. Interestingly enough, this project established the "prototype" for this kind of construction and the palette of material and colors. The design approach was a direct evolution of discussions with the client. Naturally, worked was carried out in close cooperation with the contractor to further develop the concept, build within the given budget and deliver a distinctive signature building that would bring to fruition the client's vision.

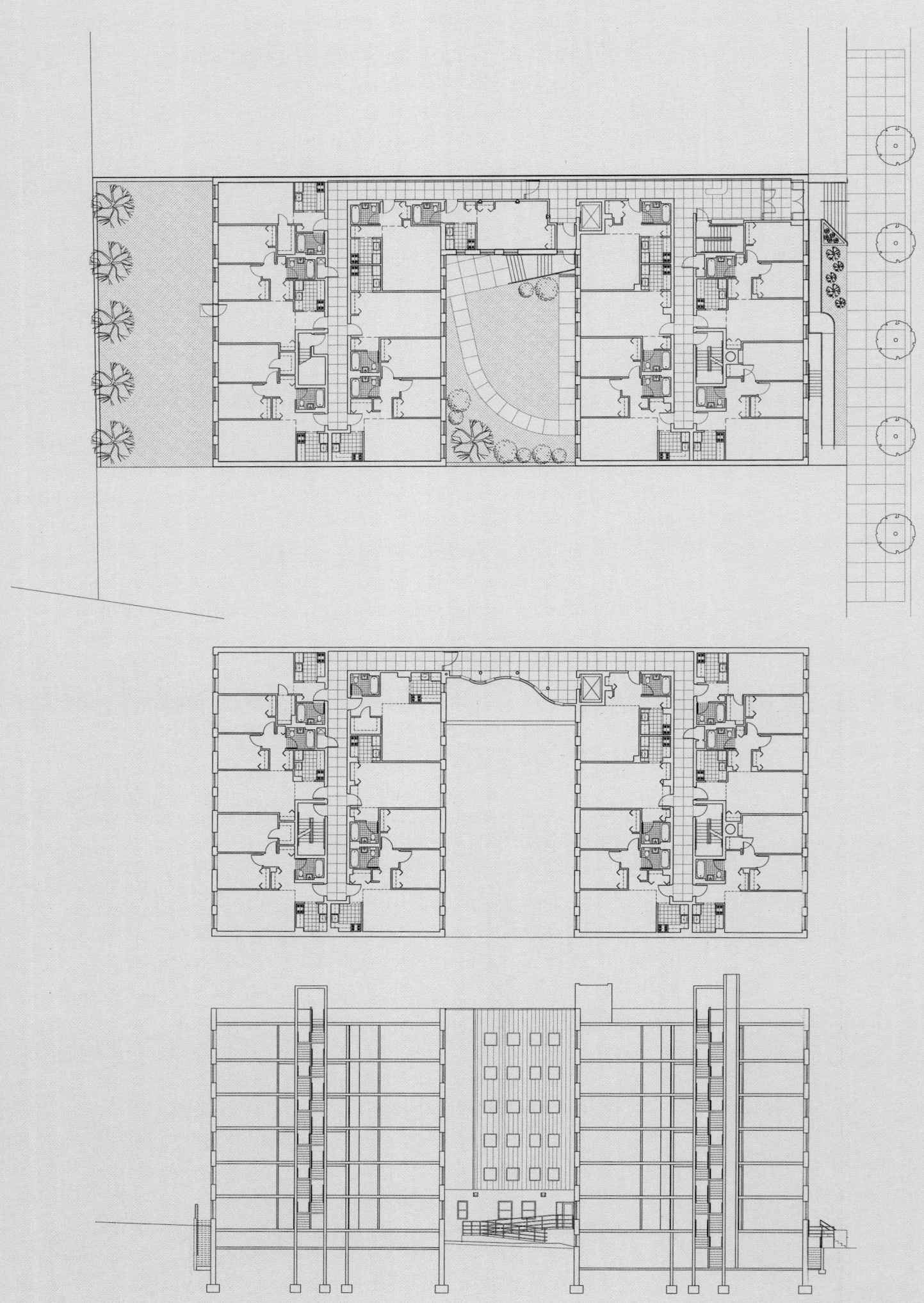

Above from top, site plan and first floor plan, showing landscaped courtyard; typical floor plan; cross section looking north.

Top, view looking north into courtyard beyond local retailers.

Above, view of front façade looking west.

43

351 East 61st Street
New York, NY

Completion Date
1999

Owner/Developer
Davis & Partners/Metropolitan New York Coordinating Council on Jewish Poverty

Architects
Meltzer/Mandl Architects, P.C.

Principal Architect
Marvin H. Meltzer, AIA, NCARB

Project Manager
Fariba Makooi

Consultants
Structural Engineer
De Simone Consulting Engineers, PLLC

Mechanical Engineer
Cosentini Associates

Photography
Christopher Lovi

TECHNICAL DATA

Square Footage
57,000

Number of Stories
15

Number of Units
53

Framing System
Cast in place concrete columns and flat slab.

Exterior Finishes
Prefabricated metal stud panels surfaced with brick and Exterior Insulation and Finish System (EIFS).

Exterior Waterproofing
EDPM roofing with pitched insulation.

Vertical Transportation
Two geared traction automatic elevators.

H.V.A.C.
Individually controlled fin-tube radiators; central gas fired boiler and domestic hot water.

Interior Partitions
Two hour fire rated gypsum drywall 50 STC between apartments.

Residential Interior Finishes
VCT floors, painted gypsum drywall, hollow metal door-frames with hollow core wood doors, textured paint for ceiling treatment, ceramic tile bathroom floors and tub surroundings.

Public Corridor Finishes
VCT flooring with painted gypsum drywall, ceiling mounted light fixtures, marble saddle and vinyl base.

Residential Lobby Finishes
Quarry tile flooring with quarry base, painted gypsum drywall and recessed down lights.

Security and Fire Protection
Line voltage smoke detectors in units.

Using New York City's "Inclusionary Zoning," this project provides a mix of 14 studio, 34 one-bedroom and five two-bedroom apartments, ranging from 640 to 1,190 square feet. A ground floor and cellar community space provide dining, recreation and health services for residents. By building this project and turning ownership over to a non-profit housing organization at completion, the developer will receive a bonus equaling four times the square footage of the building. The square footage of approximately 225,000 square feet can be applied to the developer's new market-rate housing projects elsewhere in the community. The nonprofit organization, in this case, will use the building as rental units for low- and moderate-income seniors.

The 15-story, 57,000-square-foot building design uses a poured-in-place, flat-slab structure enclosed with lightweight prefabricated panels of brick and EIFS. The prefabricated panels were manufactured in a factory in Pennsylvania, transported by truck to the site, lifted into place by crane and welded to a continuous steel angle bolted to the concrete structure.

Besides being a cost-effective solution, the panels facilitated the construction of the building. Material and labor shortages have occurred as a result of New York City's building boom; using the prefabricated panels, we were able to avoid problems sometimes associated with the masonry trade.

The front façade panels blend three colors of brick into a field of dark brick with accents of light and darker brick. The steps from the sixth floor to the building entrance feature a brick pattern that complements the decorative piers and caps. The piers and different brick colors repeat at the upper floor parapets of the front façade.

The east, west and north façades are enclosed with varying sizes of EIFS panels in blue, yellow or green pastels, creating a unique graphic pattern that coordinates with the front façade brick treatment. This approach enhances the lot line walls which, because of adjacent low buildings, are visible from the street. We have succeeded in making them visually appealing, and have avoided large, blank, windowless surfaces that would contribute nothing to the urban fabric.

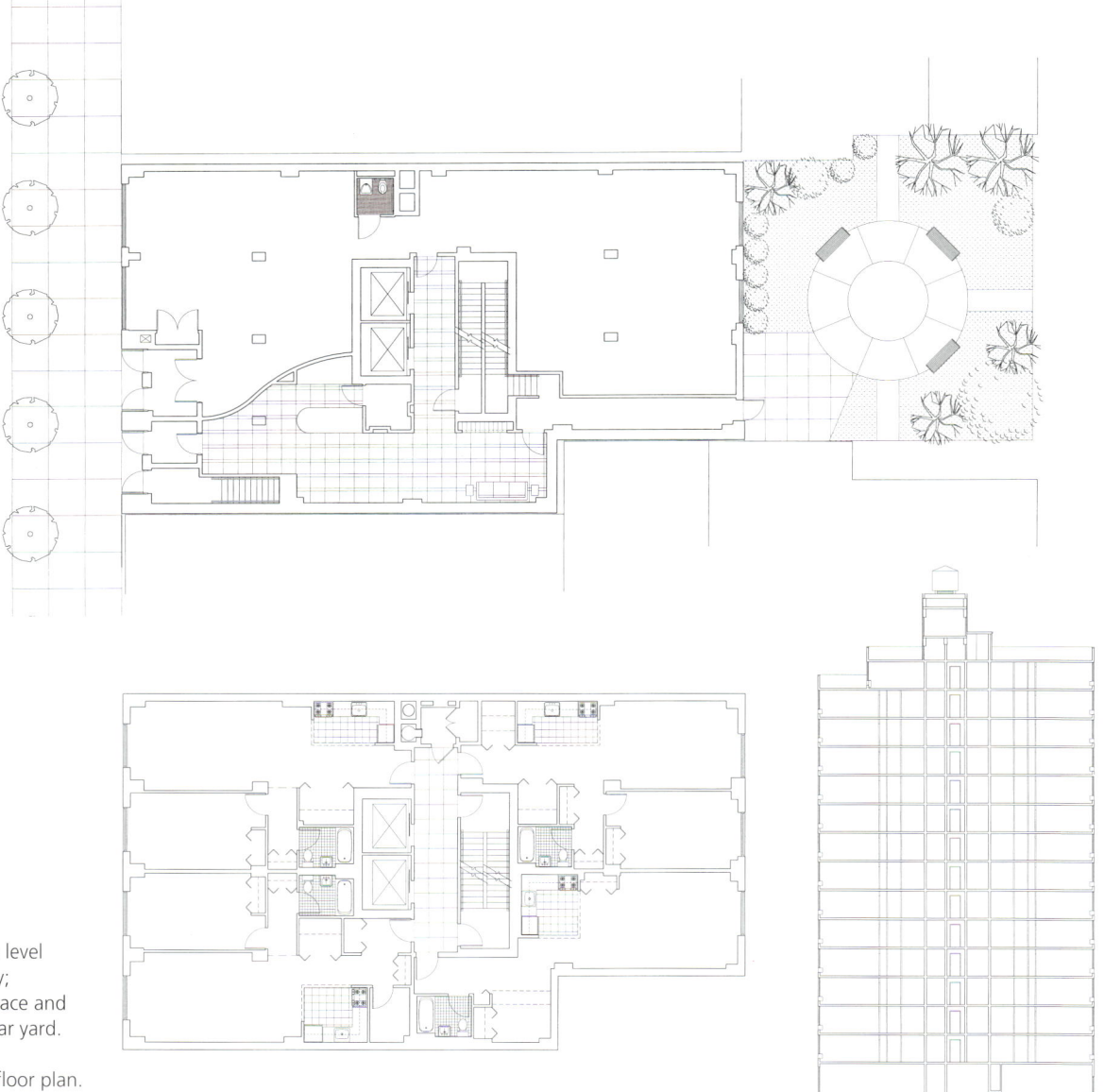

Above, first floor/entrance level showing lobby; community space and landscaped rear yard.

Right, typical floor plan.

Far right, cross section.

Top, view looking south showing colored EIFS panels at east party wall.

Opposite page, view looking north showing colored brick panels and colored EIFS panels.

Gerard Court and River Court
Bronx, NY

Completion Date
2000

Owner/Developer
Leewood Real Estate Group/The Related Companies

Architects
Meltzer/Mandl Architects, P.C.

Principal Architect
Marvin H. Meltzer, AIA, NCARB

Project Manager
Fariba Makooi

Consultants Structural Engineer
Gilsanz Murray Steficek LLP

Mechanical Engineer
Alan R. Schwartz, P.E., Consulting Engineers

TECHNICAL DATA

Square Footage
250,000

Number of Stories
Four buildings total; two 7-story
and two 3-story buildings.

Number of Units
126

Framing System
Load bearing CMU walls with pre cast concrete plank slab.

Exterior Finishes
Brick and masonry cavity walls with thermally insulated windows.

Exterior Waterproofing
Modified bitumen roofing with tapered insulation.

Vertical Transportation
Hydraulic elevator for the tower building.

H.V.A.C.
Individually controlled fin tube radiators, central gas-fired boiler and domestic hot water.

Interior Partitions
Two hour fire rated gypsum drywall, 50 STC between apartment units.

Residential Interior Finishes
Wall-to-wall carpeting, vinyl composite tile flooring in kitchens, ceramic tiles in the bathrooms and tub surroundings.

Public Corridor Finishes
Quarry tiles with painted gypsum board and painted wood chair rail.

Security and Fire Protection
Hand reader entrance doors, closed circuit security cameras in the yard, parking lot and entrance, smoke detectors in units.

Gerard Court — on a huge vacant lot near Yankee Stadium — was originally designed as Phase One of a multi-phase development that would be replicated on the site if it proved successful. It consists of three buildings connected around a landscaped courtyard. One enters the courtyard by passing through the main entrance, which is seven stories high and provides a point of security for all apartments. Two three-story buildings, designed as town houses, project off the main building. These townhouse-like units have their own entrances from the secure, landscaped courtyard. The 103,000-square-foot main structure has 126 units, of which 9 are studios, 54 one-bedroomed and 66 two-bedroomed.

Because an active elevated railroad track runs directly adjacent to the site to the west, a sound-attenuation wall was incorporated into the project, along with other techniques to reduce the impact of the noise. In addition, the wall visually blocks the lower part of the railroad trestle and offers security from River Avenue.

The challenge presented here was to create a design that would be complete at Phase One (Gerard Court) but that would also be a unified whole if and when Phase Two (River Court) were built. To further complicate the design challenge in connecting the phases, Gerard Avenue slopes down to the corner of 165th Street, which then slopes further down to River Avenue, the lowest point of the site.

Since the difference in street grade meant that the two buildings would connect at different street elevations and therefore present different massing issues, it was decided to delineate the brick pattern differently on the façades of each phase. Therefore, Phase One could be a complete composition if it alone were to reach completion. However, if Phase Two were to be built, the complete elevation would form a strong composition of different brick colors and cast stone, which would then reflect the grade condition at the street.

Parking, which is required by zoning, is provided between the two phases and the buildings are entered through the same point of security as the pedestrians off the street. Given the scale of the completed project, security was a major concern and something we took into account at all stages of the design process.

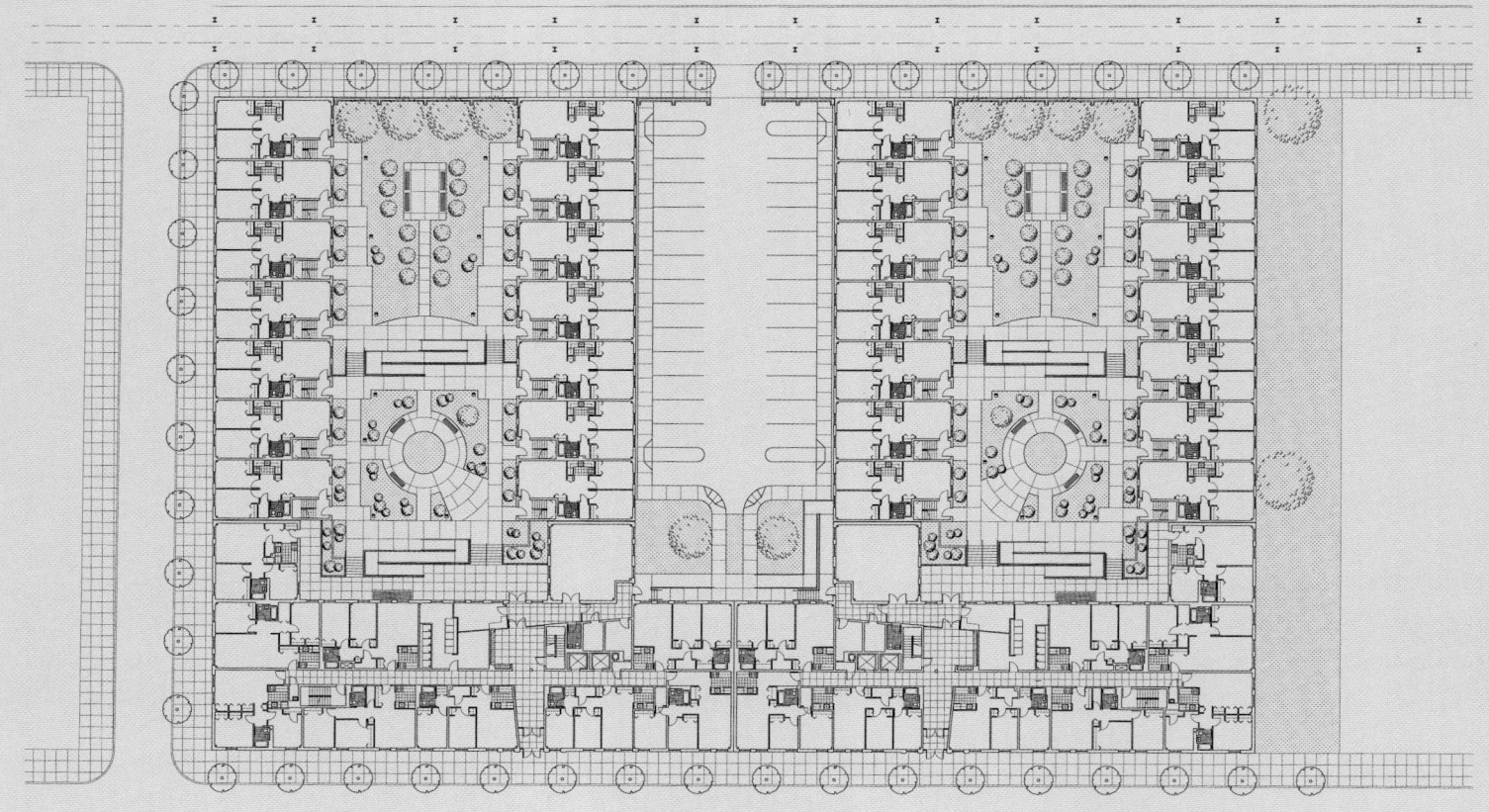
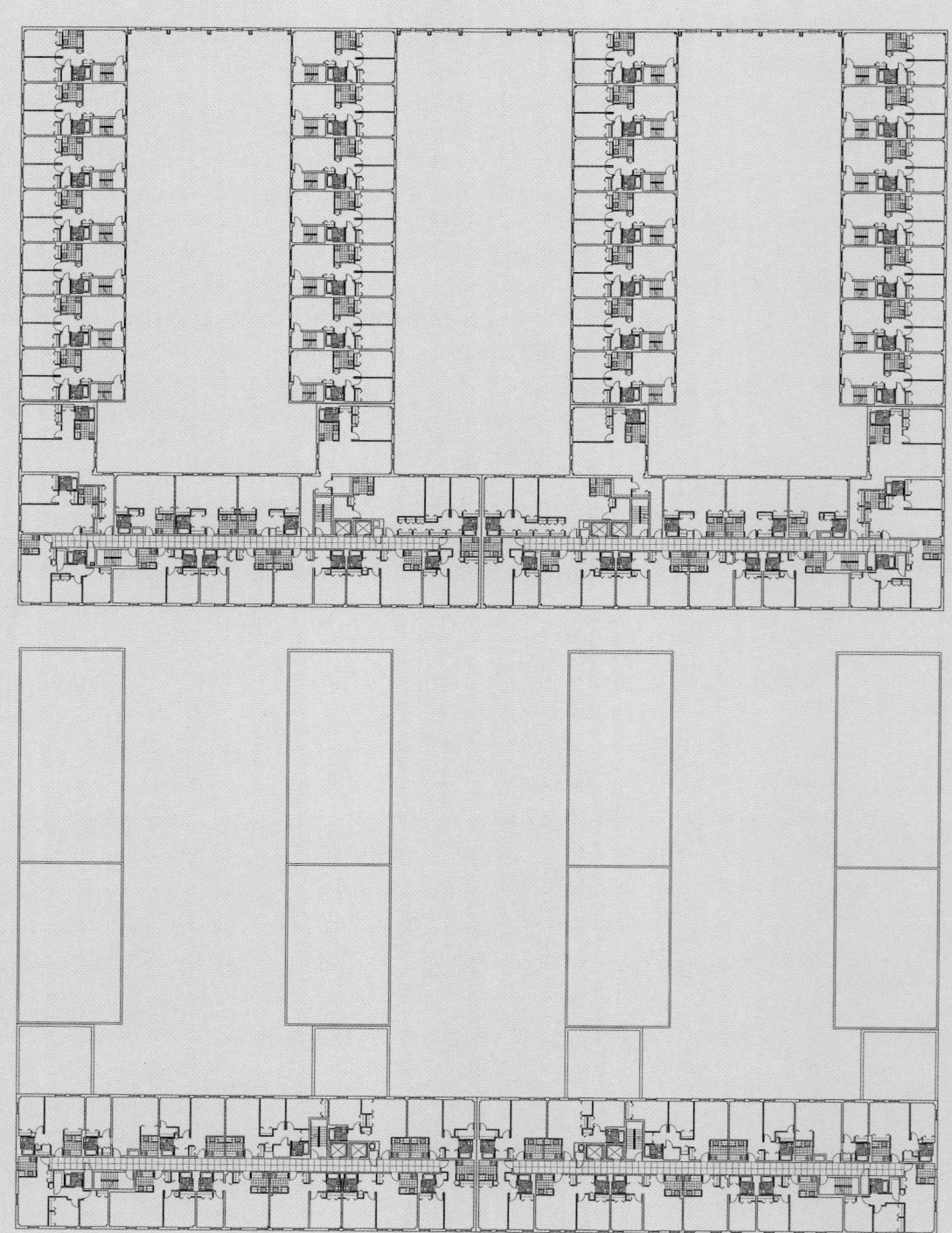

Right from top, site plan and first floor plan showing landscaped courtyards, parking and entrances to both buildings and courtyards; typical floors two and three showing apartment units and townhouse units; typical floors four thru seven of apartment towers.

Top, elevation looking north showing elevated train to the west.

Above, view of landscaped entrance courtyard for the townhouse units showing the brick and EIFS façades.

Crotona Avenue Apartments
Bronx, NY

Completion Date
2000

Owner/Developer
Atlantic Development Group

Architects
Meltzer/Mandl Architects, P.C.

Principal Architect
Marvin H. Meltzer, AIA, NCARB

Project Architect
Dan Heyden

Consultants Structural Engineer
Robert Silman Associates, P.C.

Mechanical Engineer
Alan R. Schwartz, PE, Consulting Engineers

Photography
Christopher Lovi

TECHNICAL DATA

Square Footage
72,600

Number of Stories
9

Number of Units
86

Framing System
Precast concrete plank, masonry bearing wall, precast concrete lintels.

Exterior Finishes
Three colors of brick, three colors of Exterior Insulation Finishing System (EIFS).

Vertical Transportation
One electric traction elevator.

H.V.A.C.
Individually controlled fin-tube radiators; central gas fired boiler and domestic hot water.

Interior Partitions
Two hour fire rated gypsum drywall 50 STC between apartments.

Residential Lobby Finishes
Quarry tile flooring with quarry base and painted gypsum drywall.

Residential Interior Finishes
VCT flooring, painted gypsum drywall, hollow metal door-frames with hollow core wood doors, textured paint for ceiling treatment, ceramic tile bathroom floors and tub surroundings, majority of units with awning windows in kitchen.

Public Corridor Finishes
Three colors of VCT flooring and vinyl base with painted gypsum drywall and parged CMU, ceiling mounted light fixtures.

Security and Fire Protection
Line voltage smoke detectors in units.

Additional Information
Quality Housing zoning, rear and community room courtyards, public corridors with natural light.

Crotona Avenue Apartments sits on a busy corner lot that has two different zoning categories and therefore different height, setback and massing requirements. The zoning issues were the major impetus for the design direction. Within 100 feet from the corner, it was possible to maintain the maximum building height allowed under the zoning regulations. Beyond the 100 feet from the corner, however, the height and setback requirements change, and these changes were conformed to by articulating the massing differently, both in material and form. It was at this point that it was decided it would be appropriate to introduce the EIFS system to further strengthen the brick massing that occurs within 100 feet of the corner.

The west façade incorporates an angled cutout that breaks its otherwise flat surface. The cutout was created to reduce the floor area but, serendipitously, became a strong design element. Accenting brick colors highlight specific lines of windows. A small courtyard provides the community room with valuable outdoor space, and also maintains the street wall across to the neighboring lot line. A circular core — all the way to the roof — contains the elevator and mechanical bulkheads, forming a design element around which this corner building rotates.

Crotona Avenue Apartments is the second building designed for this client and was an opportunity to expand on the criteria developed for the first project, the Carmen B. Bermudez Residence. The Crotona Avenue Apartments is another example of the expression of strong architecture achieved by creatively using a simple, rigid structural system; simple material and finishes; and brick and EIFS. The use of these materials was carefully, and clearly, defined by the client in the construction budget, and the budget was one that had to be strictly adhered to. Given the fast-track schedule in developing the project, the luxury of redesign in the event of "budget overruns" was not available. From the beginning, a complete understanding of all the construction and design issues was critical to the total success of the project.

The project was part of a government program requiring that a minimum of half of the units be two-bedroom apartments. Therefore, the building's 86 apartments are divided between studio and two-bedroom units.

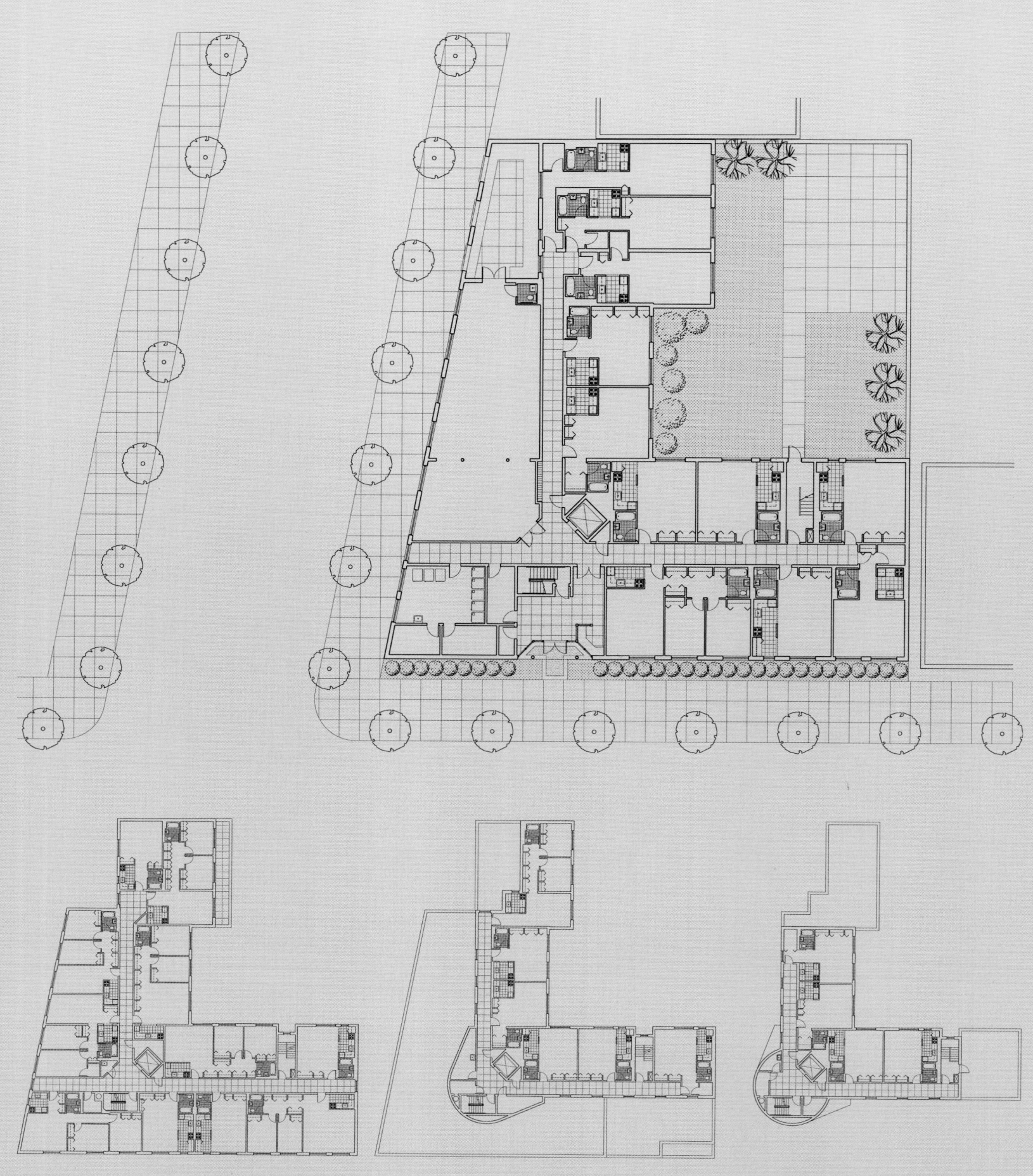

Top, site plan and first floor plan showing landscaped courtyard.

Above from left, 2nd-4th floor plans, 8th-9th floor plans.

Right from top, elevation looking east, elevation looking north, perspective looking north at entrance façade.

Right and opposite page, view looking east showing recess in exterior façade.

Below left, view looking west showing the massing which is influenced by zoning and the colored EIFS at the rear courtyard.

Below right, detail at top of building showing mechanical space and brick pattern.

Jennings Street Apartments
Bronx, NY

Completion Date
2000

Owner/Developer
Atlantic Development Group LLC

Architects
Meltzer/Mandl Architects, P.C.

Principal Architect
Marvin H. Meltzer, AIA, NCARB

Project Architect
Dan Heyden

Consultants
Structural Engineer
Robert Silman Associates, P.C.

Mechanical Engineer
Alan R. Schwartz, PE, Consulting Engineers

Photography
Christopher Lovi

TECHNICAL DATA

Square Footage
70,800

Number of Stories
6

Number of Units
84

Framing System
Masonry bearing wall, precast concrete plank and precast concrete lintels.

Exterior Finishes
Three colors of brick and three colors of EIFS are used on the façade.

Vertical Transportation
One hydraulic elevator.

HVAC
Individually controlled fin tube radiators, central gas fired boiler and domestic hot water.

Interior Partitions
Two hour fire rated gypsum drywall 50 STC between apartments.

Residential Interior Finishes
VCT flooring, painted gypsum drywall, hollow metal door-frames with hollow core wood doors, textured paint for ceiling treatment, ceramic tile bathroom floors and tub surroundings, majority of units with awning windows in kitchen.

Public Corridor Finishes
Three colors of VCT flooring and vinyl base with painted gypsum drywall and painted CMU, ceiling mounted light fixtures.

Residential Lobby Finishes
Quarry tile flooring with quarry base and painted gypsum drywall.

Security and Fire Protection
Line voltage smoke detectors in units.

Additional Information
Quality Housing Zoning, exposed rock at courtyard, natural light in public corridors.

The Jennings Street Apartment project is unique in covering the entire block front between Vyse and Hoe Streets. During the design phase of the building, the property was adjacent to a large piece of what was still vacant land. Before construction of this project was finished, a development of two- and three-family houses, which are far below the allowable density for the neighborhood, commenced construction on the vacant site.

The rear of the building sits on a huge rock outcropping that was incorporated as part of the outdoor courtyard environment. Also, since there were now going to be low-rise units on the adjacent site, a colorful and dynamic EIFS composition was used for what would be a very visible and important façade in the community. The firm had previous experience using a palette of brick and EIFS, since Jennings Street Apartments was the third affordable housing project designed in the Bronx for this same client. The criteria were the same for the previous two projects — Carmen B. Bermudez, and Crotona Avenue Apartments — so it was obvious that brick and EIFS would be appropriate; in this case, more detail was added while simplifying the color pattern.

Under applicable zoning regulations, the Jennings Street façade had to maintain a designated street wall height, so there were no mandated height and setback restrictions that could be used as design tools to provide significant articulation of the façade. Therefore, the decision was taken to interrupt the strong, consistent street façade by introducing a curved form to identify the community space at the top of building. This form successfully gives movement to the façade, expresses a difference in program and accentuates the building's entrance.

The building has 84 units: 42 studio and 42 two-bedroom apartments.

Caption

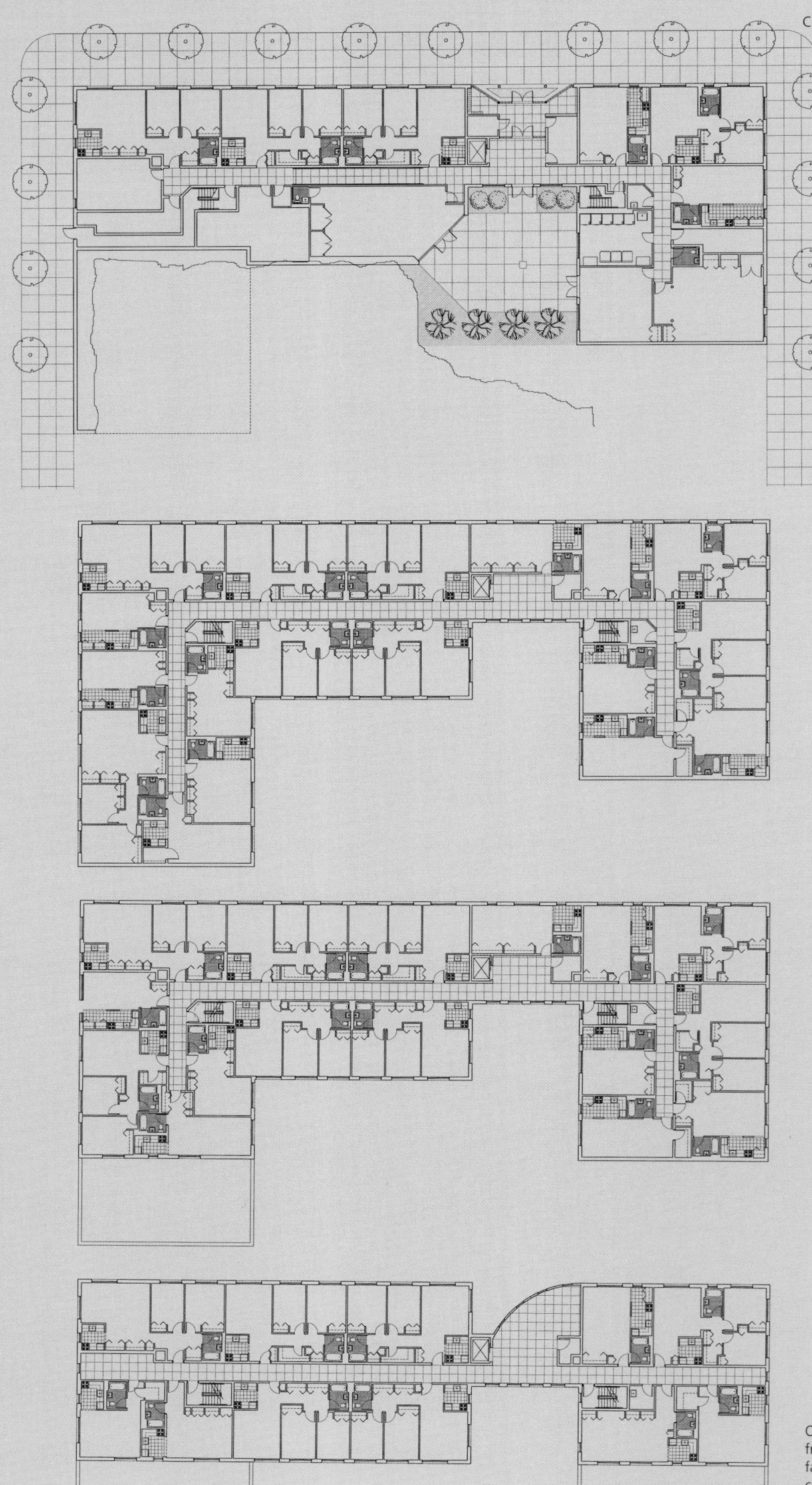

From top,
site plan and
first floor plan,
2nd-3rd floor plans,
4th-5th floor plans,
6th floor plan.

Opposite page
from top, elevation
facing north showing
composition of brick and
EIFS, elevation facing
west, perspective looking
southwest.

Top, aerial view looking north showing rear façade with EIFS colors, and low-rise neighbors under construction.

Above, view of Jennings Street façade.

Opposite page, detail view of façade in rear courtyard showing composition of EIFS colors.

Intervale Avenue Apartments
Bronx, NY

Completion Date
2000

Owner/Developer
Atlantic Development Group LLC

Architects
Meltzer/Mandl Architects, P.C.

Principal Architect
Marvin H. Meltzer, AIA, NCARB

Project Architect
Dan Heyden

Consultants
Structural Engineer
Robert Silman Associates, P.C.

Mechanical Engineer
John A. DiBari Consulting Engineers

TECHNICAL DATA

Square Footage
61,600

Number of Stories
7

Number of Units
68

Framing System
Precast concrete plank, masonry bearing wall, precast concrete lintels.

Exterior Finishes
Three colors of brick, three colors of Exterior Insulation Finishing System (EIFS).

Vertical Transportation
One hydraulic elevator.

HVAC
Individually controlled fin tube radiators, central gas fired boiler and domestic hot water.

Residential Interior Finishes
VCT flooring, painted gypsum drywall, hollow metal door-frames with hollow core wood doors, textured paint for ceiling treatment, ceramic tile bathroom floors and tub surroundings.

Public Corridor Finishes
Three colors of VCT flooring and vinyl base with painted gypsum drywall, ceiling mounted light fixtures.

Security and Fire Protection
Line voltage smoke detectors in units.

Additional Information
Quality Housing Zoning, landscaped Rear Courtyard, natural light in public corridors.

Another corner in the Bronx, subject to two different zoning categories, is the site of Intervale Avenue Apartments. The design criteria for the project were quite familiar, since it was the fourth building designed for the same client. Once again, the challenge was to design a unique, exciting, living environment in the Bronx. Unlike that of the other boroughs, the rocky, hilly landscape of the Bronx offers many odd-shaped sites and opportunities for introducing interesting forms. Intervale Avenue Apartments was no exception.

The building's long, gently curving façade follows the street's property line and is reminiscent of many of the elegant masonry façades found in the Bronx. Again, the architect's palette was brick and EIFS. Because the brick pattern provided more detail to the top floor, it was decided to simplify the pattern of colored EIFS. The different zoning categories mandated a variety of heights on the street façade. This ultimately worked out favorably, for it gave considerable strength to the massing.

The building is organized around an exterior courtyard for use by the tenants. This exterior space became very important to the project, for it is a protected outdoor space where tenants can interact with their neighbors and bring their children to play. In the building, it was possible to make use of the natural light of the outdoor space as part of the entrance lobby, thereby making both areas more exciting.

The project contains 68 units: 17 studios, 17 one-bedroom and 34 two-bedroom apartments. Previous projects for this client had shown a need for more one-bedroom apartments and fewer studios. However, in this case, 50 percent of the total units had to be two-bedroom apartments; of the remaining units, half are studios and the other half one-bedroom units.

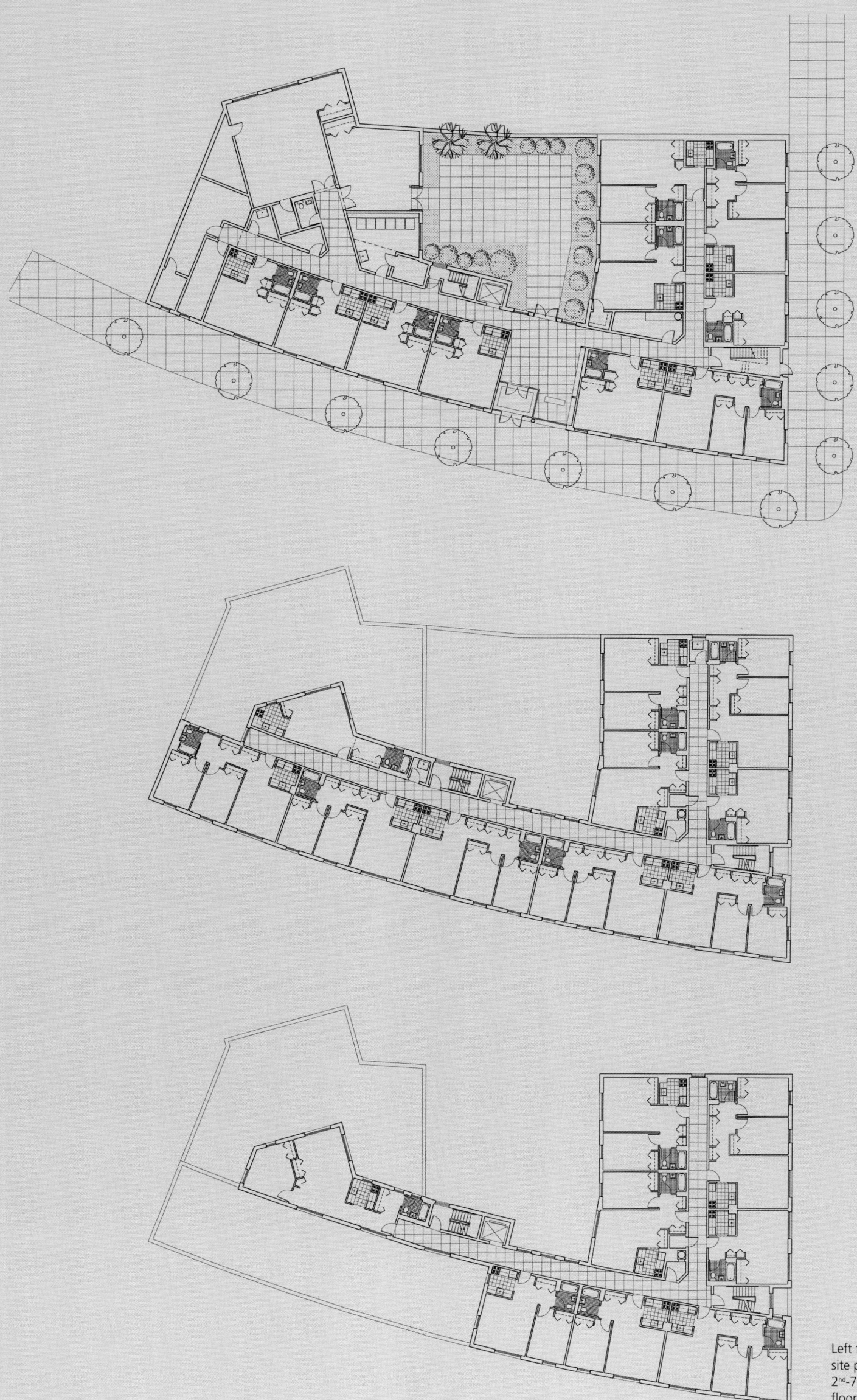

Left from top,
site plan and first floor,
2nd-7th floor plans, 8th-9th floor plans.

Top, view looking east at front elevation.

Above, view looking north toward from front façade showing colors and patterns of brick and EIFS.

67

Bradhurst Court
New York, NY

Completion Date
2002

Owner/Developer
Bradhurst Development Company, LLC.

Architects
Meltzer/Mandl Architects, P.C.

Principal Architect
Marvin H. Meltzer, AIA, NCARB

Project Manager
Dan Heyden

Consultants
Structural Engineer
The Office of James Ruderman, LLP

Mechanical Engineer
John A. Di Bari Consulting Engineers

TECHNICAL DATA

Square Footage
260,000

Number of Stories
8

Number of Units
126

Framing System
Structural steel and metal deck up through the 2nd floor. Precast concrete plank, masonry bearing wall, precast concrete lintels above.

Exterior Finishes
Three colors of brick, three colors of Exterior Insulation Finishing System (EIFS).

Vertical Transportation
Two electric traction elevators.

H.V.A.C.
Individually controlled fin-tube radiators; central gas fired boiler and domestic hot water.

Interior Partitions
Two (2) hour fire rated gypsum drywall 50 STC between apartments.

Residential Lobby Finishes
Quarry tile flooring with quarry base and painted gypsum drywall.

Residential Interior Finishes
Parquet flooring, painted gypsum drywall, hollow metal door frames with hollow core wood doors, marble tile bathrooms and tub surrounding, slate flooring in the kitchens with stone counter tops, ceiling mounted light fixtures in foyers and corridors.

Public Corridor Finishes
Carpet, vinyl wall covering, ceiling mounted fluorescent light fixtures, marble saddles.

Security and Fire Protection
Closed circuit security cameras in courtyard, entrance & garage, line voltage smoke detectors in units.

Additional Information
Garage below grade, supermarket at 1st floor, courtyard with condominium townhouses and community room at 2nd floor, 1BR, 2BR, and 3BR condominiums above. Quality Housing zoning, public corridors with natural light.

Bradhurst Court is an affordable home ownership and commercial development in Harlem's Bradhurst neighborhood. This 260,000-square-foot development represents a major part of Harlem's ongoing urban renaissance. One-, two-, and three-bedroom apartments and duplex townhouses comprise the 126 residential units. The major retail component is a 45,000-square-foot, value-oriented supermarket that will encompass the entire site at street level. A 49,000-square-foot parking garage below grade will serve both the retail and residential components of Bradhurst Court.

The development takes up an entire Manhattan city block, bounded to the north and east by two major thoroughfares—West 145th Street and Frederick Douglas Boulevard—and on the South and West by 144th Street and Bradhurst Avenue. An approximately 18-foot drop in grade runs from the high corner of 145th Street and Bradhurst to 144th Street and to Frederick Douglas Boulevard. This grade became, by far, the most significant element in the design scheme. First, it allowed an entrance to the supermarket to be designed at street level on Frederick Douglas Boulevard, an essential requirement for the supermarket tenant. Second, the grade made it possible to develop the supermarket rooftop as an outdoor landscaped space, around which the entire scheme is organized. All residents now use the same lobby on 145th Street, and the outdoor space serves as an entrance court for the duplex townhouses at that level and as a private recreational area for the home owners. Alternatively, residents who live in apartments on the floors above can continue riding up the elevator to their homes, bypassing the courtyard. They do, however, benefit from the courtyard when looking down from their apartments: the once unsightly roof is now covered with greenery. Further, the grade allows the residents of the duplex townhouses to enter their homes directly off the street on Bradhurst Avenue and, due to the grade condition, these units could be located directly under the duplex townhouses which are entered at the courtyard level above. In response to community sentiment, the townhouses echo the look of townhouses directly across the street on Bradhurst Avenue and maintain the traditional urban character of the Bradhurst neighborhood.

Side streets lined with late 19th and early 20th century brick row houses and medium-scale, multi-family buildings suggest the fabric of the neighborhood, as do major avenues anchored by larger multi-family buildings with local businesses on the ground floor. It is precisely this scale and architectural character that has been preserved for Bradhurst Court, while still providing an opportune and exciting project that will contribute to the economic growth of this legendary New York City community.

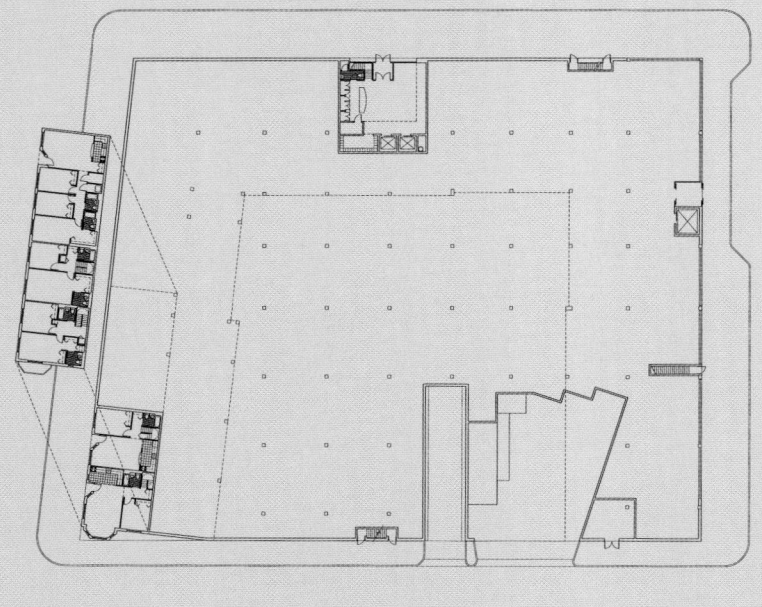
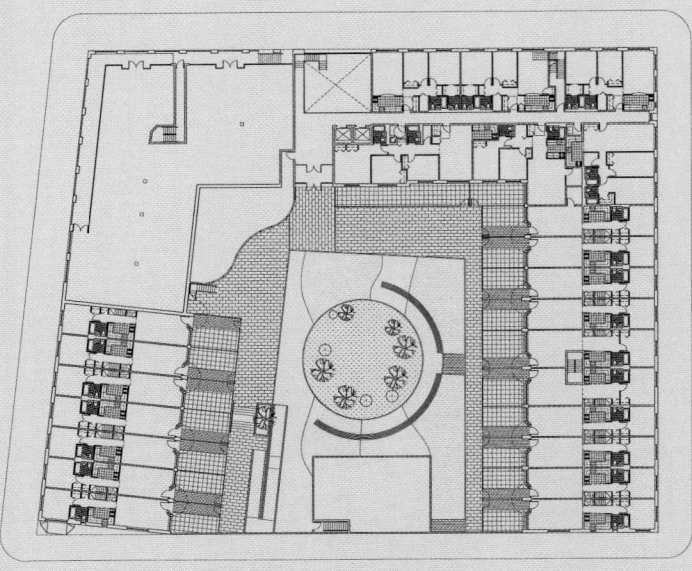
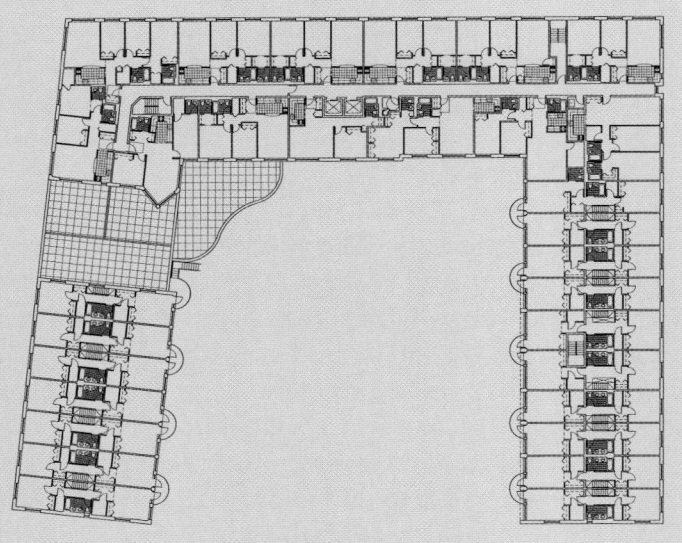
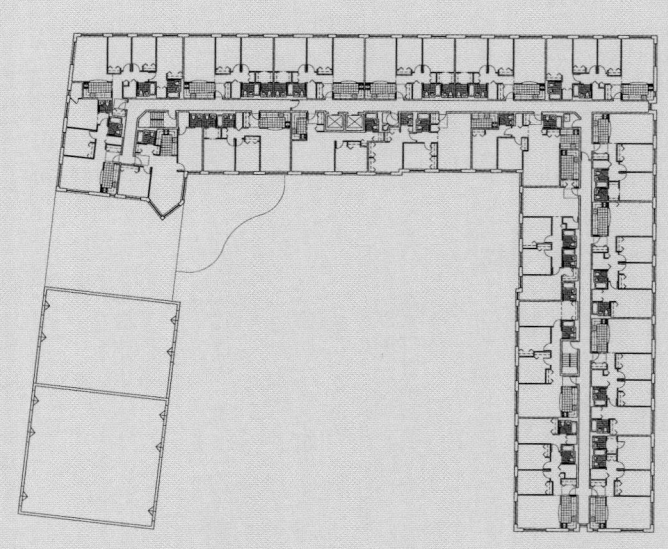
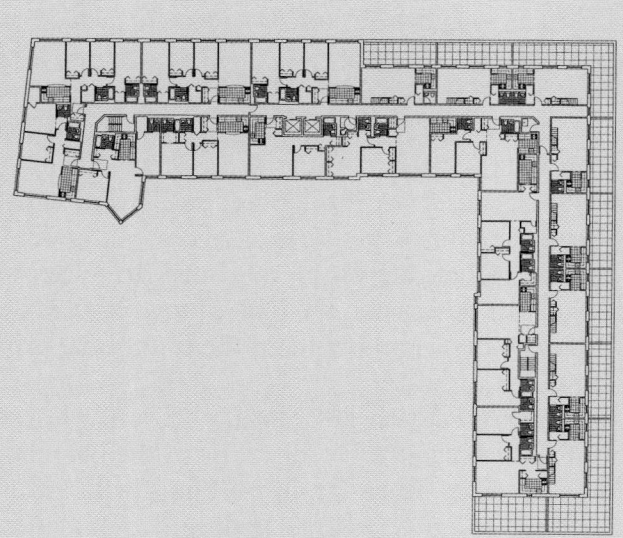
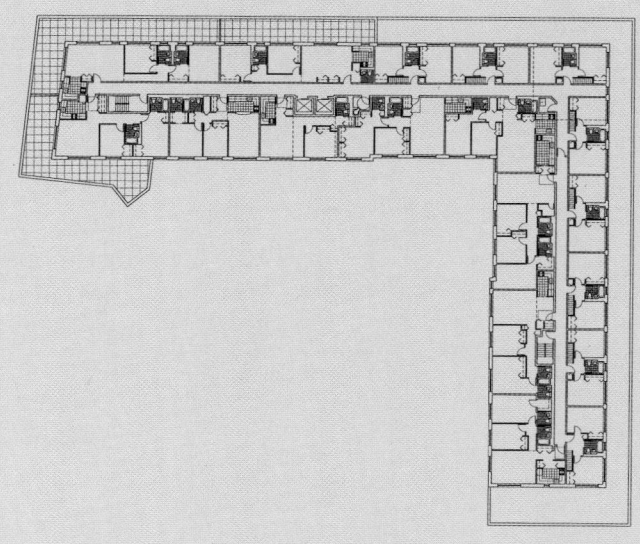

Top left, site plan and first floor plan showing supermarket, services and apartment building lobby.

Top right, second floor plan.

Middle left, third floor plan.

Middle right, 4th-6th floor plans.

Above left, seventh floor plan.

Above right, eighth floor plan.

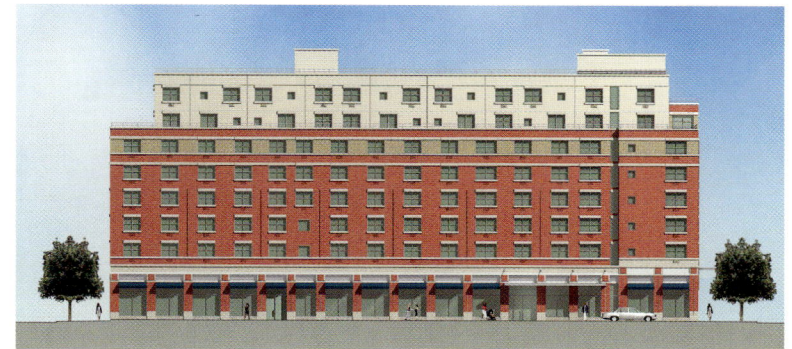

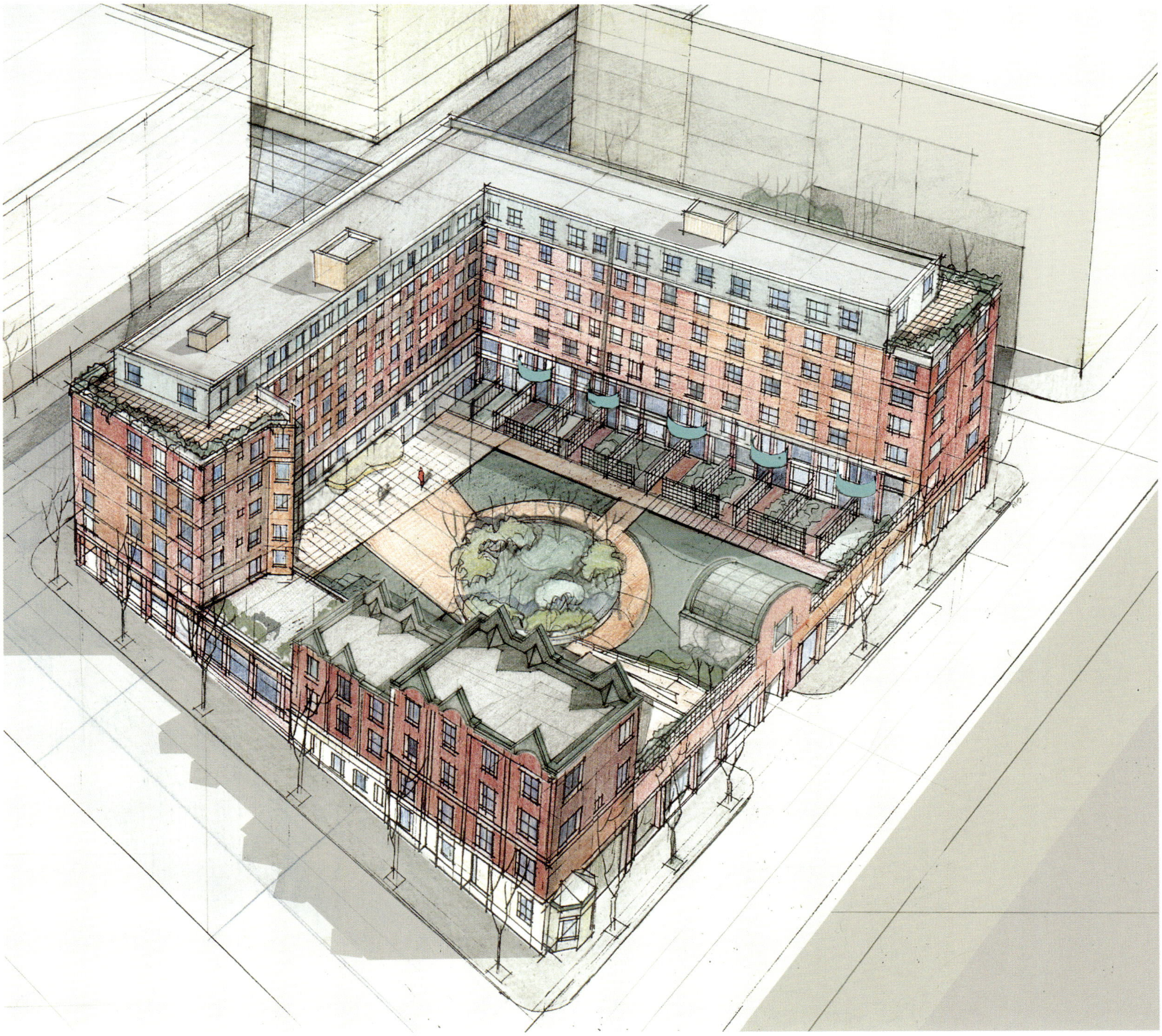

Top left, elevation along Bradhurst Street looking east showing apartment tower; retail at street level and townhouse units.

Top right, elevation looking west along Frederick Douglas Boulevard showing apartment tower and street level retail.

Above, aerial rendering of entire complex outdoor, rooftop courtyard, which serves as entrance to the duplex townhouse units.

Urban Projects

"The approach to the following urban projects" Meltzer says, "is rooted in my architect/developer career and my nonprofit experiences with government agencies. The architecture has evolved and been refined throughout the past 20-odd years. Likewise, the scale of the projects has grown with the booming economy.

As I reflect on my career, I realize that all experiences — dealing with economic considerations, specific materials, structural systems, the populations served, even the construction nightmares—ultimately became an inventory of knowledge that I drew upon with every new project. In many ways all the experiences were the same — however, the developers and owners were different, and each had different expectations of me.

Today, developers of market-rate, luxury housing are incorporating elements of affordable or low-income housing to maximize profits. When called upon, I am comfortable being their advocate when dealing with government agencies. My relationships in the for-profit and nonprofit fields enable me to move projects along efficiently and quickly. The scale of some of the projects also allows me to once again 'push the envelope' of innovation, constantly seeking ways to improve the quality of the architecture, shorten the development process and still respect my clients' budgets.

As I write this, our economy is robust. Everyone is moving faster than ever, hoping to generate new opportunities in architecture. It's exciting that over the years I have gathered the broad range of experience necessary to take advantage of these special opportunities."

306-308 East 38th Street
New York, NY

Completion Date
2001

Owner/Developer
The Clarett Group

Architects
Meltzer/Mandl Architects, P.C.

Principal Architect
Marvin H. Meltzer, AIA, NCARB

Project Manager
Fariba Makooi

Consultants
Structural Engineer
Office of James Ruderman, LLP

Mechanical Engineer
I.V. Consulting Engineers

TECHNICAL DATA

Square Footage
111,000

Number of Stories
20

Number of Units
97

Framing System
Cast in place concrete column and flat slab.

Exterior Finishes
Prefabricated lightweight metal stud panels surfaced with brick and aluminum.

Roofing
Built-up "IRMA" roofing system with pre-cast stone panels.

Vertical Transportation
Two geared traction automatic elevators.

H.V.A.C.
Individually controlled packaged terminal air conditioners, gas fired boilers, domestic hot water.

Interior Partitions
Two (2) hour fire rated gypsum drywall with 50 STC rating between units.

Residential Interior Finishes
Parquet flooring, painted gypsum drywall, hollow metal door frames with hollow core wood doors, marble tile bathrooms and tub surrounding, slate flooring in the kitchens with stone counter tops, ceiling mounted light fixtures in foyers and corridors.

Public Corridor Finishes
Carpet, vinyl wall covering, ceiling mounted fluorescent light fixtures, marble saddles.

Security and Fire Protection
Line voltage smoke detectors in units.

Additional Information
Cantilevering of the west façade over an adjacent 5-story building.

Located on East 38th Street between Second and Third Avenues, this new 20-story, 104,000-square-foot luxury residential rental project is a neighbor to other high-end luxury residential buildings on the same block. The site assembles five parcels to the west and a light and air easement to the south. Among several unique features is the architectural approach and treatment of its façades. Above the second floor, the building is sheathed with an attractive combination of brick and Alucobond (aluminum) lightweight prefabricated panels (hung on a typical flat slab concrete frame), giving it a distinctive presence. The building's base of slate supports an intriguing glass and stainless steel canopy. Twelve stories of the west façade cantilever over an adjacent 5-story building, offering yet another interesting attraction.

Upon entering the building, tenants are greeted by the soothing sound of moving water from a fountain wall in the lobby. The slate used on the outside of the building carries through with complementary shades of green on the inside, forming the fountain wall as well as the floor and other walls surfaces of the lobby. A concierge desk stands out as an important element in a lobby that pulls materials of stainless steel and stone together eloquently.

With a maximum of six units per floor, there is a feeling of intimacy not often available in rental building properties. The building's top six floors feel even more special, for there are only four apartments per floor. At the 15th floor, the building steps back to create wonderful apartments with terraces.

The building has 97 units with a mix of studio, one-bedroom, and two-bedroom apartments. Six units are designed as duplexes to maximize the number of apartments having roof terraces. The apartment layouts and generous fenestration take advantage of expansive views to the east, south and west. Some of the larger units are designed with eating alcoves next to the kitchen. All units feature washers and dryers and microwave ovens; in addition, they are cable-ready and wired for high-speed Internet access. Finishes include a pleasing combination of wood parquet floors in the living room, dining room and bedrooms; marble floors and walls in the bathrooms; and marble floors and granite counter tops in the kitchen. All units are designed for handicapped adaptability.

Among the common amenities are a health club, an event space on the ground floor and an outdoor recreation area on the roof. On the ground and cellar floors of the building, 3,400 square feet is available for medical office suites.

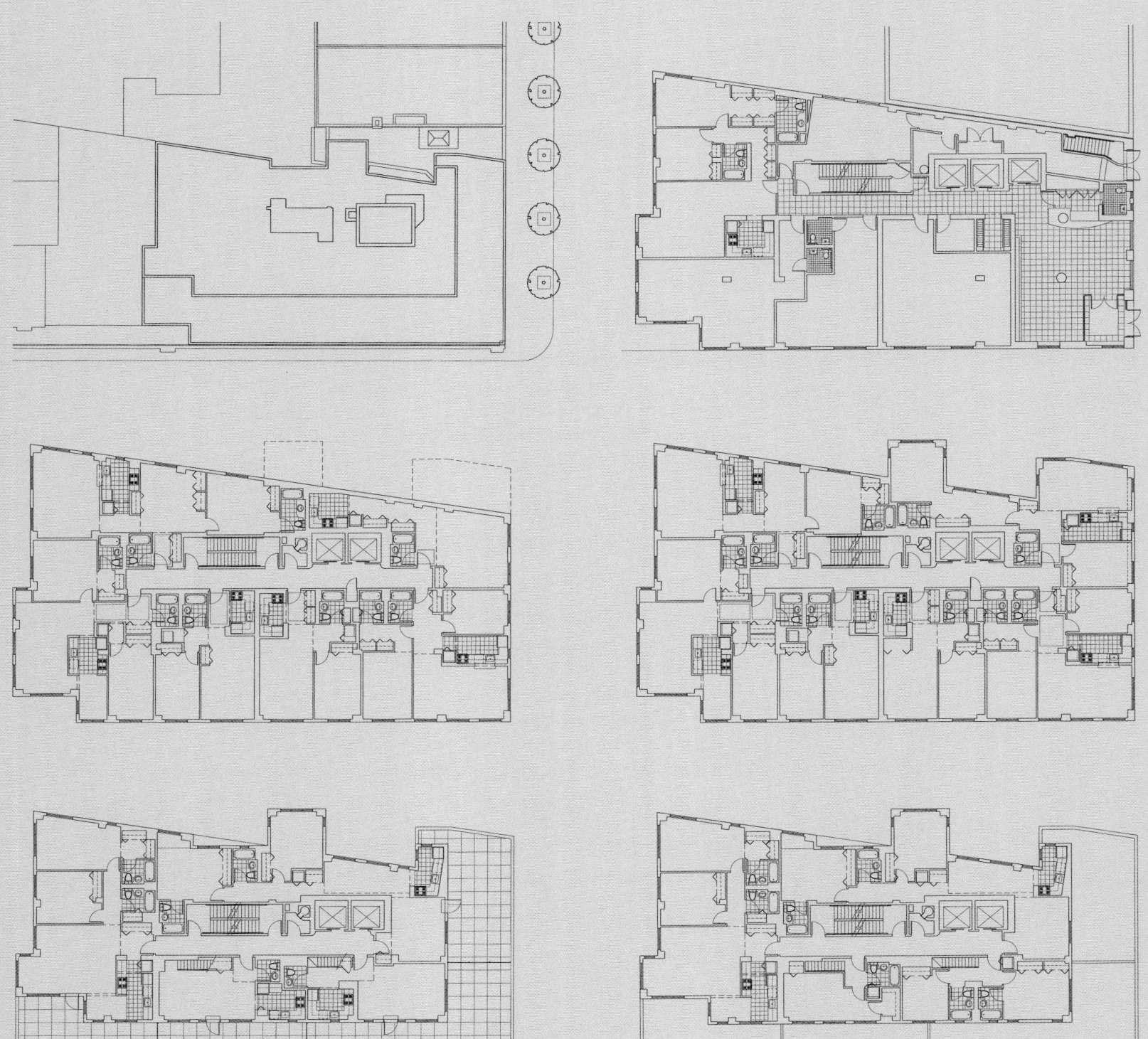

Top left, site plan.

Top right, first floor plan showing residential lobby entered off East 38th Street.

Middle left, 2nd-8th floor plan.

Middle right, 9th-14th floor plan.

Above left, 15th-17th-20th floor plans showing lower level of duplexes.

Above right, 16th-18th-19th floor plans showing upper level of duplexes.

Right, view looking north.
The skin is light-weight prefabricated panels faced with brick tile, aluminium panels, and stone.

Park Avenue Sephardic Congregation
New York, NY

Completion Date
In design

Owner/Developer
Park Avenue Sephardic Congregation

Architects
Meltzer/Mandl Architects, P.C.

Principal Architect
Marvin H. Meltzer, AIA, NCARB

Project Manager
Yu Inamoto

TECHNICAL DATA

Framing System
Cast in place concrete column and flat slab.

Exterior Finishes
Brick and block non-load bearing cavity wall, thermally insulated windows on side and rear walls. Granite façade and aluminum and glass curtain wall at street wall.

Vertical Transportation
Two geared traction automatic elevators.

H.V.A.C.
Individually controlled heat pump units, central gas fired boilers and domestic water.

Interior Partitions
Two (2) hour fire rated gypsum drywall with 50 STC rating between rooms.

Interior Finishes
Carpet floor, painted gypsum drywall, hollow metal door frames with hollow metal doors, marble tile bathrooms, ceiling mounted light fixtures in corridors.

Corridor Finishes
Carpet, vinyl wall covering, incandescent accent light, slate saddle and wall base.

Security and Fire Protection
Line voltage smoke detectors.

Lobby Finishes
Combination of wood, marble and wall covering; cove lighting with pendant fixtures.

A 13-story, 30,000-square-ft. synagogue and school are planned for the south side of a busy midtown block, along with seven floors that accommodate a co-ed high school.

The two-story main sanctuary will seat 400 worshipers; a smaller mezzanine chapel seats 50. The synagogue program includes a 3,000-square-foot social hall with kitchen facilities, private dining club, conference rooms, a full-height cellar gymnasium and a rooftop indoor swimming pool. The school facilities are on the fourth to tenth floors.

The front façade of the tall, thin building has a glass wall above the third floor where a Jewish star is inlaid in a powerful but subtle way. The star deliberately starts above the third floor to avoid being blocked by traffic on this congested street. A glass and metal roof allows natural light to enter the pool area at the top of the building. Since there are no tall buildings on either side of the site, it was easy enough to introduce windows on the side façades to provide a brighter environment for the classrooms. Although these windows are not valid for purposes of legal light and air requirements, the windows offer a very pleasant amenity in midtown Manhattan.

Here again, the massing of the building is almost entirely defined by the zoning envelope. Interpreting that zoning, it was possible to inject a strong sense of identity to a newly formed congregation in the middle of Manhattan.

Having grown up in a strong Jewish tradition where the synagogue culture was a very important part of my youth, I personally viewed this project as an opportunity to reconnect with my earlier life. At the heart of it, I wanted to contribute something meaningful to the Jewish community in New York City and to the architectural fabric of Manhattan. A new building such as this one is unique today, particularly in the midst of a commercial midtown neighborhood. My goal was to design a building that was traditional and contemporary, religious in feeling, yet respectful of its diverse neighbors, and a bright, welcoming symbol that the congregation could be proud of.

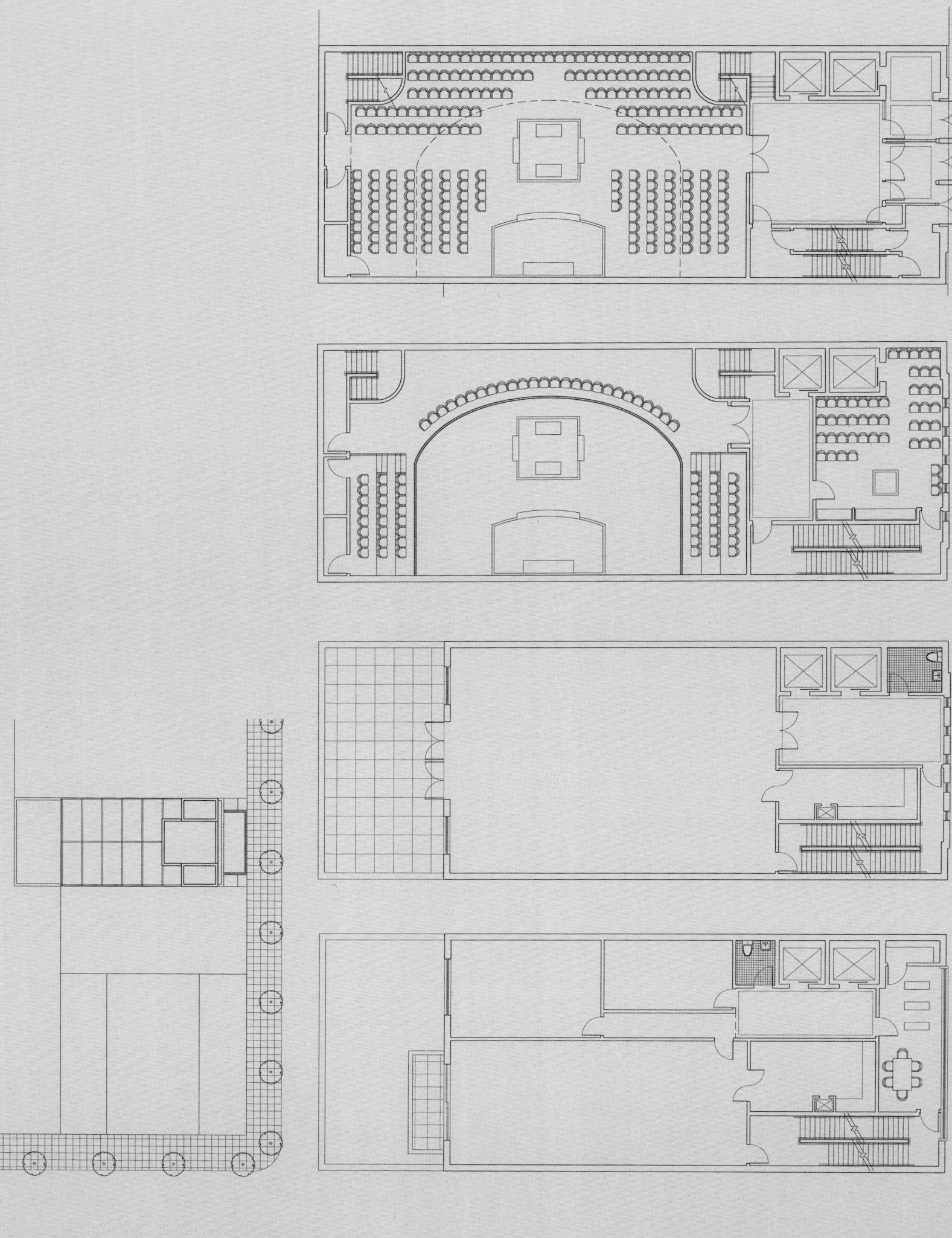

Above from top, floor plans: first floor showing sanctuary, mezzanine level – chapel, second floor plan – social hall; third floor plan.

Above, site plan.

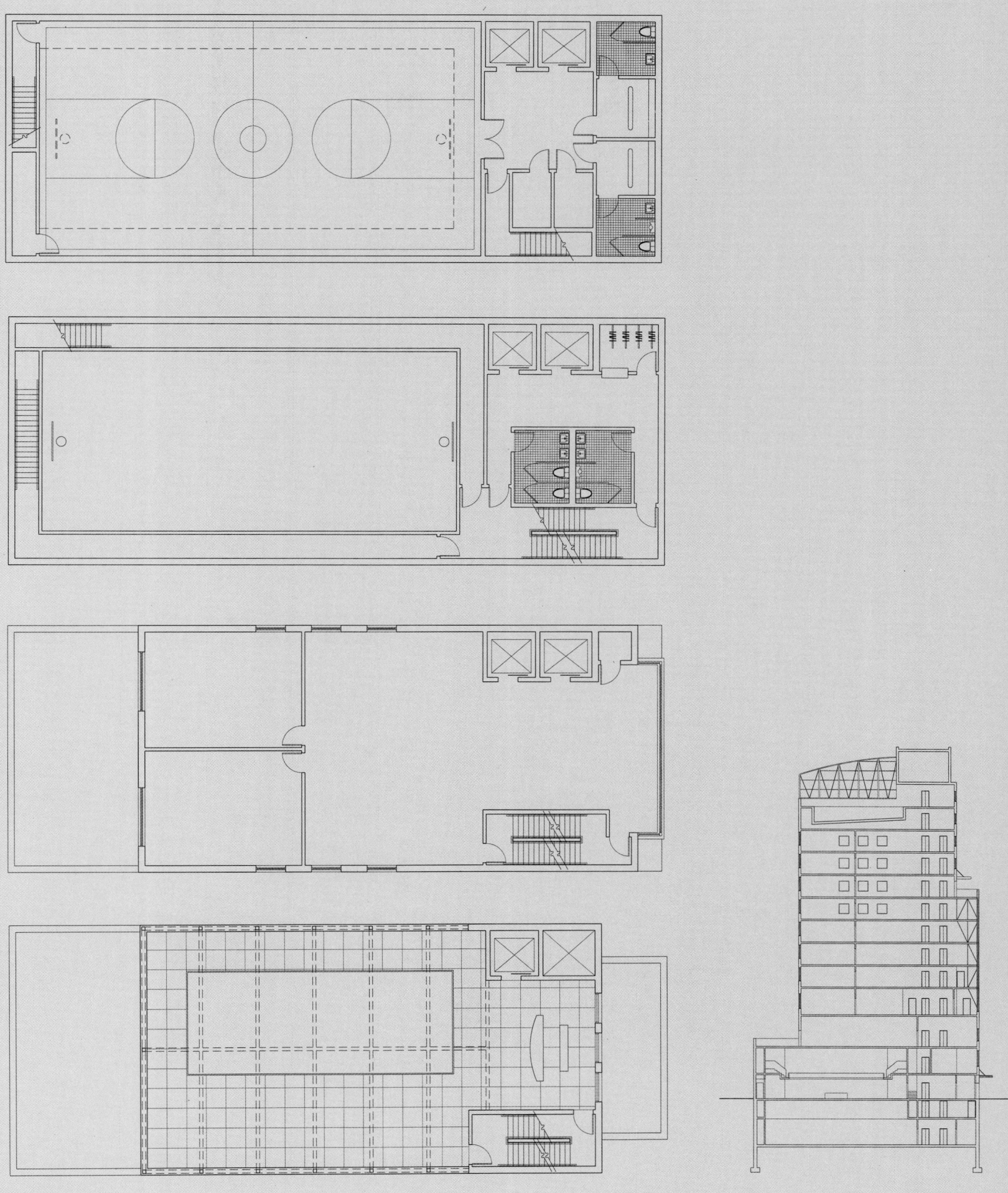

Above from top, lowest level plan showing gymnasium; gymnasium mezzanine level, typical floor plan 4th-10th, pool level plan.

Above, cross section looking west.

81

Above, elevation looking west showing glass enclosed pool at top floor.

Opposite page, front elevation.

83rd Street and York Avenue
New York, NY

Completion Date
2001 – in design

Owner/Developer
The Somerset Group

Architects
Meltzer/Mandl Architects, P.C.

Principal Architect
Marvin H. Meltzer, AIA, NCARB

Project Manager
Yu Inamoto

TECHNICAL DATA

Square Footage
190,000

Number of Stories
33

Number of Units
141

Framing System
Cast in place reinforced concrete columns and flat plate slab.

Exterior Finishes
Brick and block non-load bearing cavity wall, thermally insulated windows at residential levels. Aluminum and glass store front at first floor level, granite façade at main entrance.

Exterior Waterproofing
Built-up pre "IRMA" type roofing system with gravel and/or precast stone pavers.

Vertical Transportation
Geared traction automatic elevators.
H.V.A.C.
Individually controlled fan coin units, central oil fired boilers and domestic hot water.

Interior Partitions
Two (2) hour fire rated gypsum drywall, 50 STC between apartment units.

Residential Interior Finishes
Hardwood floors, painted gypsum board drywall, hollow metal door frames, wood doors, kadex ceiling treatment, ceramic tile kitchen floors and bathroom floors and tub surrounds.

Public Corridor Finishes
Carpet, vinyl wall covering, incandescent accent light, slate saddle and wall base. All materials class "A" flame spread.

Residential Lobby Finishes
Slate floors, wood, slate and metal walls, fluorescent cove lighting and incandescent spot lighting.

Security and Fire Protection
Doorman, closed-circuit television and electrically activated door strike at fenced plaza and residential entry vestibule, line voltage smoke detectors in units.

This 33-story, 190,000-square-foot luxury residential tower sits on the corner of East 83rd Street and York Avenue, on Manhattan's Upper East Side. The site covers four assembled parcels and utilizes square footage obtained from air rights from adjacent buildings to the south. From the upper portion of the tower, one has views in all directions and can readily take in the East River and midtown Manhattan.

The building juxtaposes two distinct characters: the six-story base of brick and stone, and the slender tower that climbs up to the sky as brick slowly disappears and glass and spandrel panels wrap the facades. On the tower's upper portion are several slim vertical recesses that add a jewel-like quality to the façade as seen from the street. The use of stone and brick at the building's base creates a sense of mass and foundation for the tower.

The first floor's spacious entrance lobby leads to a conference room and community room, which face a peaceful courtyard with a fountain. The rest of the first floor is occupied by 2,900 square feet of medical offices as well as a ramp to an attended parking area with two levels for underground parking.

Since the building was intended for the high end of today's market, apartments are arranged strategically to accommodate the neighborhood's particular demand. All of the apartments feature large living rooms with superb views and natural light, kitchens with adjacent dining/breakfast areas by the window and comfortable bedrooms with plentiful storage space.

Floors two through six have two studio and seven one-bedroom apartments per floor. The lower portion of the tower, floors seven through 24, has on each floor one three-bedroom apartment and three two-bedroom apartments, ranging from 1,100 square feet to 1,500 square feet. The upper portion of the tower has three three-bedroom apartments per floor, ranging from 1,500 square feet to 1,700 square feet. The top floor offers penthouse apartments with roof terraces. On the south side of the roof are a garden and swimming pool.

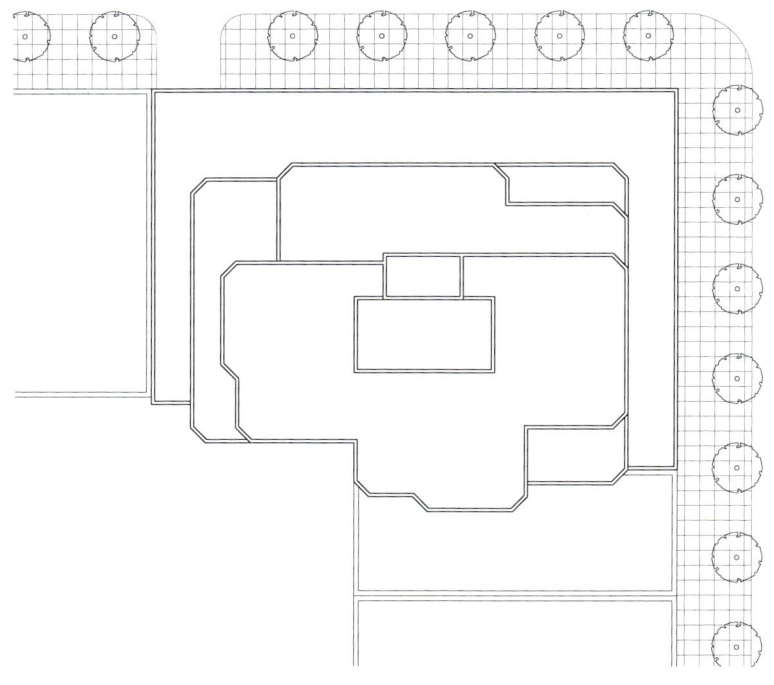
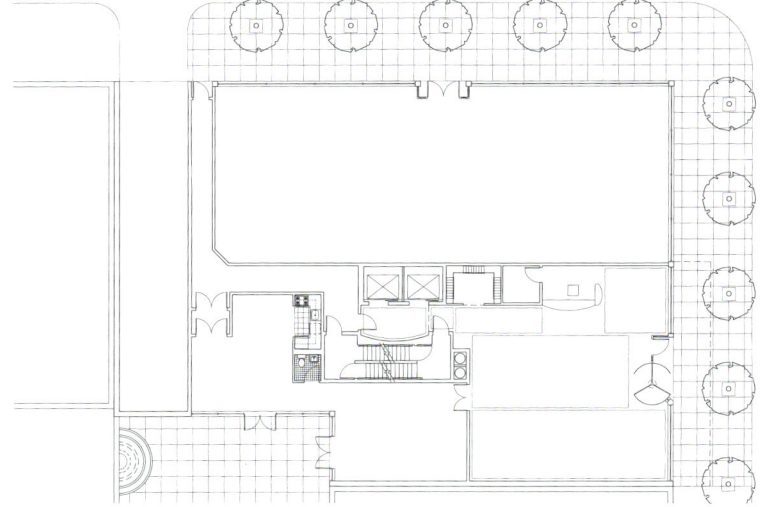
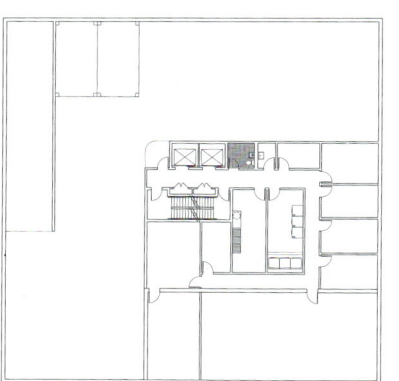
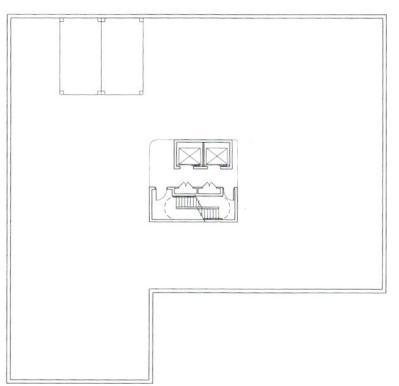

Above, York Avenue elevation looking west.

Right from top, site plan, first floor plan showing residential lobby and commercial space, cellar floor plan showing garage and services, sub cellar floor plan showing garage.

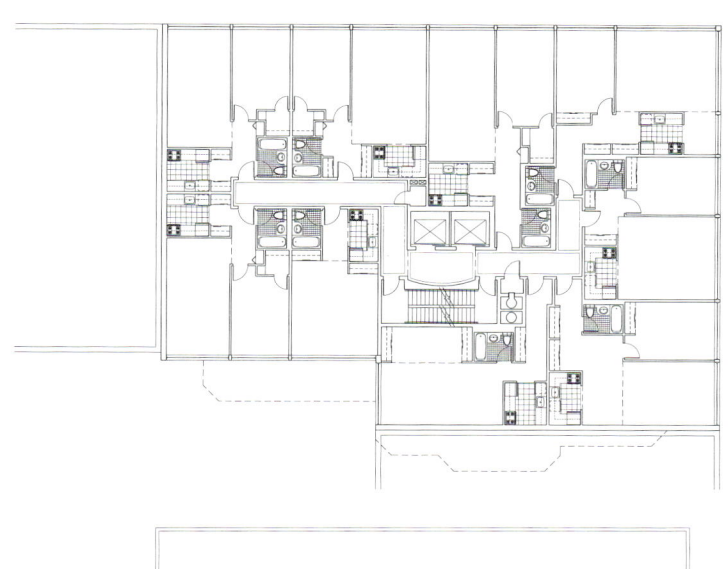
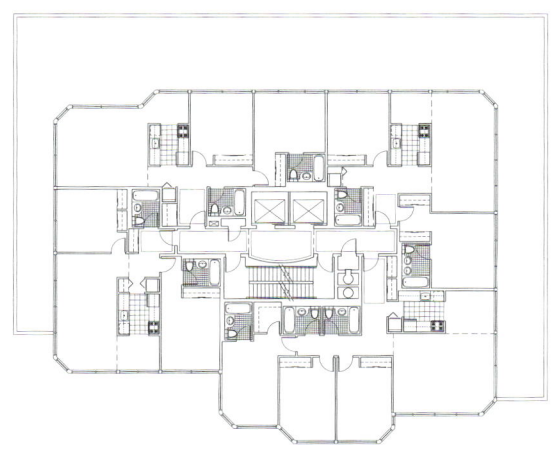
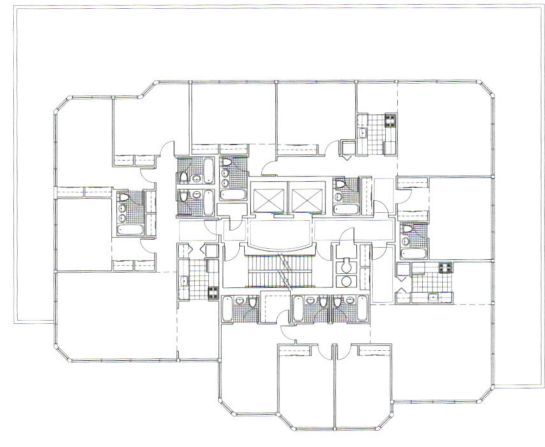
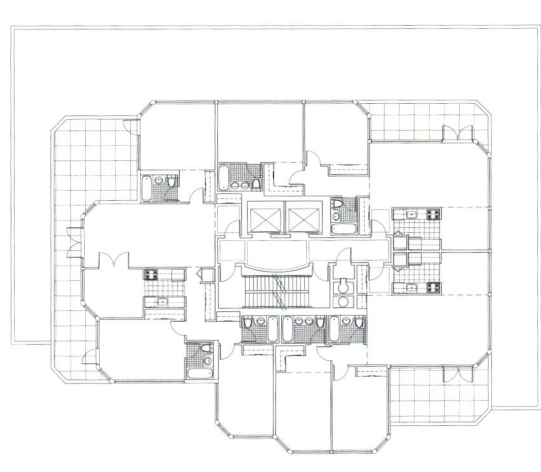
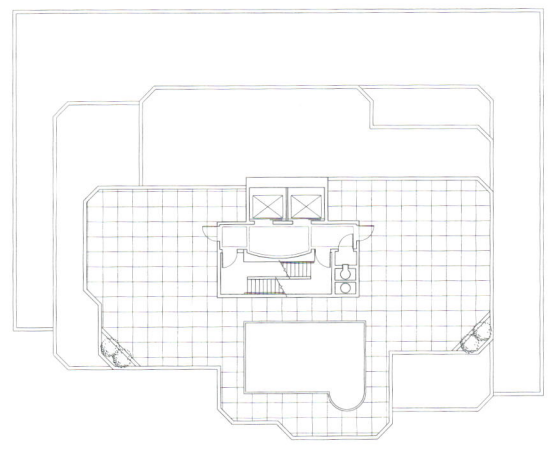
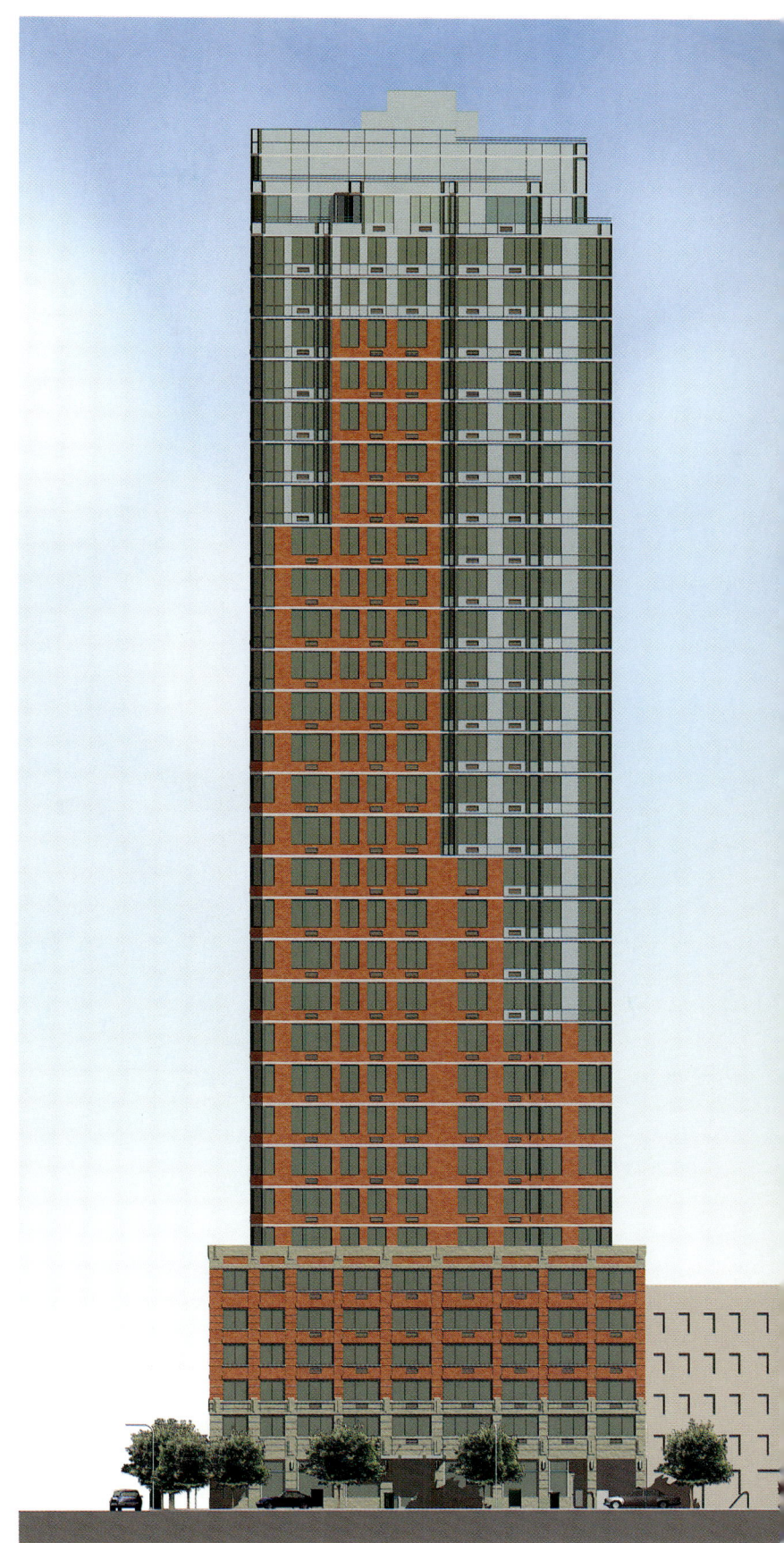

Left from top,
2nd-6th floor plan, 7th-24th floor plan, 25th-31st floor plan, 32nd floor plan, roof top/pool level plan.

Above, 83rd Street elevation looking south.

87

Queens West Development Project

Long Island City
Queens, NY

Design Date
2000

Owner/Developer
Time Equities, Inc.

Architects
Meltzer/Mandl Architects, P.C.

Principal Architect
Marvin H. Meltzer, AIA, NCARB

Project Architect
Yan Meng

TECHNICAL DATA

Site
24 Acres

Recreational Parkland
7 Acres

Square Footage
2.6 million

Number of Stories
Ranges from 4-50 Stories

Number of Residential Units
2,500

Number of Parking Spaces
2,000

Queens West Development rises on a 24-acre waterfront site in Long Island City in the borough of Queens. Situated on the banks of the East River, it will comprise three distinct neighborhoods that will be built during four development stages. The client, who is interested in purchasing the stage II site, asked for a schematic design to be drawn up for possible presentation to the governing municipal agencies involved in the project and to Pepsi-Cola, which owns the waterfront site.

Several requirements had to be catered for. The scheme had to (1) emphasize a major park space for active outdoor recreational use, (2) maximize the number of units (among 2,500) that will enjoy the truly superb views of Manhattan, (3) include a small amount of retail space in the development, and (4) conform to a road pattern established in an earlier master plan of all four phases of Queens West Development. In fact, while the road pattern was not altered, a new massing scheme was introduced to respond to the special qualities of the site.

To create the recreational park, the scheme opted for the area between Center Boulevard (the main road) and the East River, thus offering park users exciting views of Manhattan. A unique element for the park space was the preservation of the lighted Pepsi-Cola sign, a New York landmark for more than 30 years. The owners felt that the image itself, approximately 45 feet in height and 145 feet in length, will work well into the new century. To preserve the image and to relocate it to its most advantageous spot, a small baseball stadium was designed with a facade to support the Pepsi-Cola sign. The image recalls methods of advertising in small baseball parks of the past. At its new location, the sign will be entirely visible from Manhattan and will not block any residential views from Queens West.

Four residential towers were placed over by the eastern side of the site. Three of the towers rise out of four-story bases, each of which includes a parking garage. The towers are situated to maximize the views of Manhattan. A striking, 50-story elliptical glass tower at the north end of the site is the focal point of the complex. This building will have spectacular views in all directions: Manhattan to the west; the Queensboro Bridge to the north; the Brooklyn and Manhattan Bridges to the south; and Queens and Long Island to the east.

The towers' four-story bases are enclosed by two levels of townhouse units. Some townhouses can be entered directly from both the street and the park, a particularly desirable feature in New York City. The other townhouses have entrances off an open, landscaped court. Additional duplex units are accessible from the main lobby of the towers.

As part of the scheme, our goal was to create a strong street facade along one side of Center Boulevard and step up the massing toward the towers. By having one tower directly face the water and Manhattan, an outdoor park space was created in the residential complex that would connect with the main recreational park over on this side of Center Boulevard. The orientation of this tower also serves to distinguish the development from existing towers on adjacent properties. The orientation also differs from buildings in the planning phase, which will be parallel with each other.

All these structures will be in a park setting accessible to pedestrians and with limited vehicle access. The exterior façades will be clad with a lightweight prefabricated panel system faced with appealing combinations of glass, brick and aluminum. The complex will offer one of the finest urban views available in the United States.

Below, first floor plan showing lower level of townhouse units and parking garage. Right from top, section/elevation looking north, plans of courtyard level above garages.

90

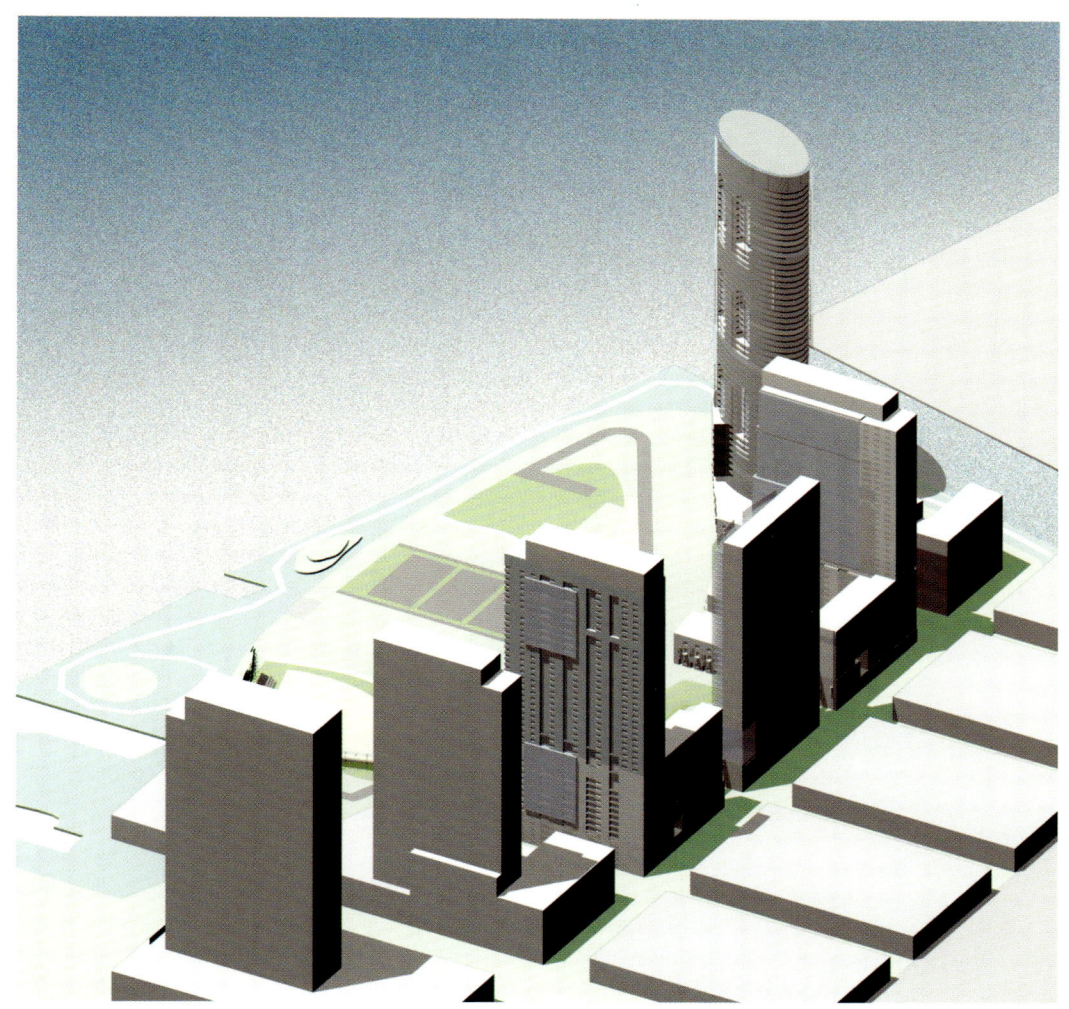

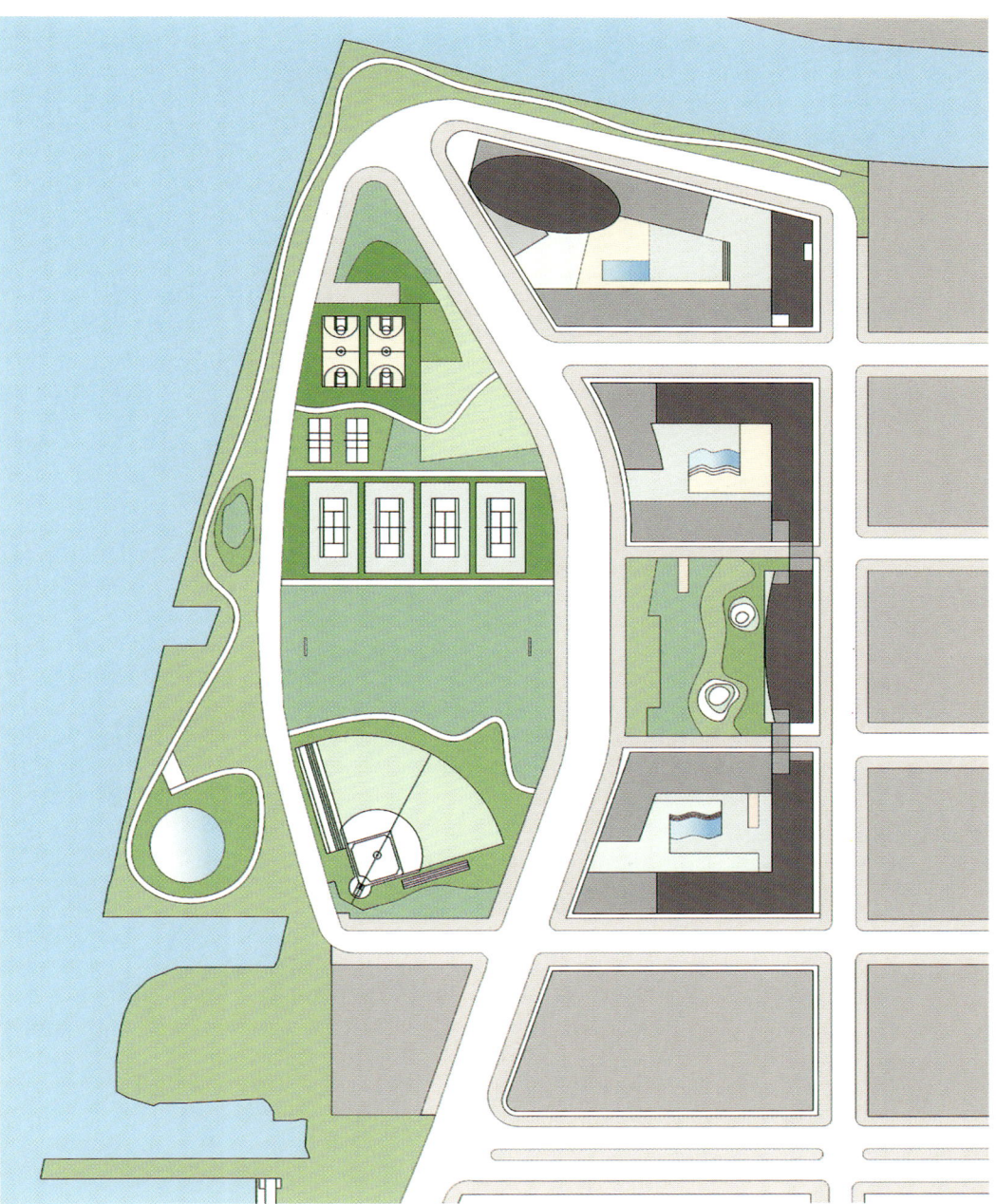

Right from top, perspective looking northwest and site plan showing park, baseball stadium and apartment buildings.

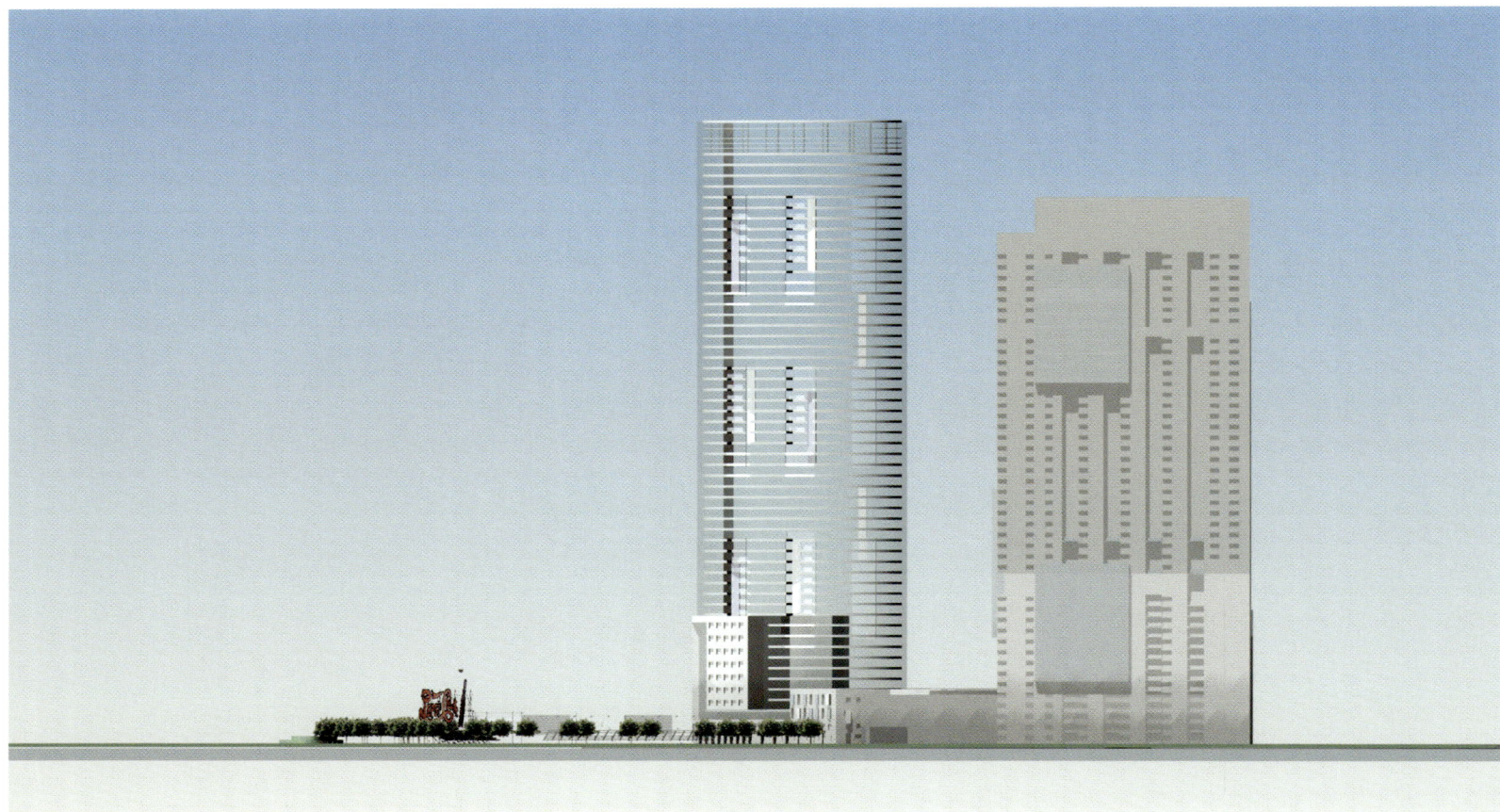

Above from top,
elevation of entire
project looking east;
elevation looking north.

Above from top, perspective rendering looking northeast showing relocation of Pepsi-Cola sign; perspective rendering looking north with view of Manhattan.

Perspective rendering looking north from park area.

Perspective rendering looking north from courtyard within residential complex.

Complete List of Works

100 West 81st Street, New York, NY
110/120 Church Street, New York, NY
130 East 30th Street, New York, NY
134 Ninth Avenue, New York, NY
21 East 23rd Street, New York, NY
220 East 25th Street, New York, NY
240 East 26th Street, New York, NY
258 West 55th Street, New York, NY
306-308 East 38th Street, New York, NY
340 East 29th Street, New York, NY
351 East 61st Street, New York, NY
420 West 23rd Street, New York, NY
45 Wall Street, New York, NY
58 West 109th Street, New York, NY
60 Broad Street, New York, NY
Artist's Residences, South Salem, NY
Atria Senior Quarters, West 86th Street, New York, NY
Banco De Brazil, New York, NY
Big Brothers/Big Sisters, East 30th Street, New York, NY
Bradhurst Court, New York, NY
Cambridge House on the Hudson, Ossining, NY
Carmen Bermudez Residence, Bronx, NY
Children's Aid Society, 20 Sullivan Street, NY
Covered Bridge Center, Manalapan, NJ
Crotona Avenue Apartments, Bronx, New York, NY
Crotona Park West, Bronx, NY
Danbury, Downtown Redevelopment
Danon's on the Park, New York, NY
Disadvantaged Children's Residence, Peekskill, NY
Doctor's Park, Smithtown, Long Island
East 25th Street, New York, NY
Fishbein, Olivieri, Rozenholc & Kunstler, New York, NY
Fordham Bedford Housing Corporation, Webster Ave, Bronx, NY
Gateway to Hopewell, VA
Gerard Court and River Court, Bronx, NY
Gold Residence, Plainview, NY
Great Neck Child Development Center, Great Neck, NY
Great Neck Parks Dept, Thomaston Park, Great Neck, NY
Greencroft Condominiums, New Rochelle, NY
Greystone Mental Hospital, Greystone Park, NJ
Hakim Residence, New York, NY
Hakim Residence, South Egremont, MA
Hartley House, West 46th Street, New York, NY
Housing & Services, Inc,
Hudson Street Townhouses, New York, NY
I.B.M. Cafeteria Building, Burlington, VT
Intervale Avenue Apartments, Bronx, NY
Jennings Street Apartments, Bronx, NY
Lawson Boulevard Office Building, Oceanside, NY
Lee Goodwin House, Bronx, NY
Lynell Medical Tech, New York, NY
Madison Square Garden – Old Site, New York, NY
Madison Square Garden Perimeter Lighting, New York, NY
Mathias Residence, New York, NY
Melrose Court, Bronx, New York, NY
Meyerhoff House, Prince Georges County, MD
Monastery Girls Residence, Archdiocese of NY
Monica House, Queens, NY
Montessori School, Edison, NJ
Mount St. Florence, Peekskill, NY
N.Y.I.T. Conference Center, Old Westbury, Long Island
Nassau County Children's Remand Home, Westbury, Long Island
Nassau County Department of Probation, Westbury, Long Island
National Football Hall of Fame, New Brunswick, NJ
New Destiny Housing Corporation, Staten Island, NY
New Directions in Community Revitalization, Bronx, NY
Oltarsh & Oltarsh, New York, NY
Park Avenue Sephardic Congregation, New York, NY
Plainview Cooperative Nursery School, Plainview, Long Island
Plutos Retreat, Long Island, NY
Postgraduate Center for Mental Health, East 86th St., New York
Professional Building, Anoka, Minnesota
Provincetown Playhouse, New York, NY
Purgess Residence, Upper Greenwood Lake, NY
Rice Street Townhouses, St. Paul, Minnesota
Rooms of Tomorrow, New York, NY
Rotunda Drawings, Traffic Circle, West 77th St. Boat Basin, NY
Rozenholc Residence, New York, NY
Sabella, New York, NY
Sojourner Truth House, Bronx, NY
Sons of Moses Congregation, St. Paul, Minnesota
South Station Development, Boston, MA
St. Christopher Episcopal Church, St. Paul, Minnesota
St. John the Baptist Monastery, New York, NY
St. John's House, Bronx, NY
St. Malachy's Day Care Center, Queens, NY
Steppingstone Park, Great Neck, NY
The Aurora, West 57th Street, New York, NY
The Enclave, East 52nd Street, New York, NY
The NorthMoore, New York, NY
The Sharing Community, Yonkers, NY
Time Equities, Inc., New York, NY
Volunteers of America, 2643 Broadway, New York, NY
Women in Need/ Shearson-Lehman Child Development Center, Bronx, NY
Women's American ORT, Inc., New York, NY

Biography

Marvin H. Meltzer was educated at the University of Minnesota in Minneapolis, where he received a Bachelor of Arts degree in 1959 and a Bachelor of Architecture degree in 1961.

In 1965, Meltzer moved to New York to join the firm of Charles Luckman Associates as a member of its design staff. He later became a project designer for the firm of Damaz & Weigel, where he worked in the areas of residential, commercial and institutional architecture. Before establishing his own practice in 1972, Mr. Meltzer was a project designer for the New York office of Curtis & Davis.

Meltzer has been a guest design critic at the University of Minnesota, Columbia University, the City College of New York, Cooper Union and the City University of New York. He is a member of the American Institute of Architects and of the National Council of Architectural Registration Boards.

Concurrent with his own architectural practice, Meltzer was co-founder and President of Britton Development, Ltd. (BDL). In this capacity, he was responsible for the direction of the architectural staff and for playing a critical role in selecting the sites and analyzing the economic and environmental practicability in each phase of BDL's development projects. He also founded BDL Construction Corporation, which built some of the development projects.

In the late 1980s, as economic conditions shifted and less private development work was taking place, Meltzer built a practice that addressed special needs and supportive housing financed with government funding. As a result, he became familiar with New York City areas that were considered less desirable, such as the South Bronx.

In 1994, as Marvin H. Meltzer Architects, P.C., Meltzer's design of Melrose Court in the South Bronx was recognized as the Best Affordable Multifamily Housing Project of the Year by the National Association of Home Builders. In his work today, Mr. Meltzer continues providing quality housing for low-income populations.

Meltzer designed the adaptive reuse of 45 Wall Street in 1996—the first large-scale office-to-residential conversion to be completed in lower Manhattan.

In 1995, Meltzer entered a partnership with David Mandl, RA, forming Meltzer/Mandl Architects, P.C.

Over the last 35 years, Meltzer has designed and developed many types of buildings and environments. His experience has included the design of luxury, affordable and special needs housing, as well as childcare, educational, community facility and commercial projects. Meltzer's philosophy is that quality design is a key factor in all projects, and he has achieved a solid track record of providing responsible, sensitive design solutions on time and within budget.

Education:
University of Minnesota
Bachelor of Arts, 1959
Bachelor of Architecture, 1961

Registration:
National Council of Architectural Registration Boards
State of New York
State of New Jersey
State of Connecticut
State of South Carolina

Affiliations:
The American Institute of Architects (AIA)
AIA New York Chapter - Housing Committee
Central Synagogue, NY - Building Committee Member

Awards:
Best Affordable Multi-Family Project
1994 Pillars of the Industry Award
National Association of Home Builders
National Council of Multi-family Housing

1995 Veteran Small Business Advocate
U.S. Small Business Administration

Periodicals:
NEW YORK TIMES *Low-Income Bronx Apartments Near Completion* 11/26/99
MULTI-HOUSING NEWS *Rehabs and Renovations* 9/99
NEW YORK TIMES *Adding Color to E. 61st Street* 9/26/99
REAL ESTATE NEW YORK *Optimism 'Reigns' on Downtown's Parade* 4/99
REAL ESTATE NEW YORK *Mining for Enhanced Value in the Tax Credit Market* 3/99
NEW YORK TIMES *Bridgemarket Emerging After 22 Years* 3/7/99
NEW YORK TIMES *A Synagogue For East 58th St.* 2/20/99
REAL ESTATE WEEKLY *MMA Designs a Complex Residential Conversion* 2/24/99

NEW YORK TIMES *Surge in Low-Income Apartments in the Bronx* 2/12/99
NEW YORK TIMES *For Tribeca, A 49 Unit Condo* 1/17/99
REAL ESTATE WEEKLY *Hughes Avenue Apartments Tops Off* 7/29/98
REAL ESTATE WEEKLY *Construction Begins on Bronx Affordable Housing* 7/15/98
REAL ESTATE WEEKLY *Leewood Begins Construction of Affordable Bronx Housing* 7/1/98
NY CONSTRUCTION NEWS *Construction Begins for Bronx Housing Units* 7/98
NEW YORK TIMES *Linking Low Rent Housing to Manhattan Market* 4/26/98
REAL ESTATE WEEKLY *The Need for Speed in Today's Developments* 1/28/98
CRAIN'S *Placement Agencies Find a Niche* 1/5/98
NEW YORK TIMES *South Bronx Revival Shifting to 2-Family Houses* 12/26/97
MULTI HOUSING NEWS *Wave of Rental Conversions in Downtown NYC Points to Architecture of Interior Spaces* 11/97
REAL ESTATE WEEKLY *Meltzer/Mandl Architects Designing Conversion of 110/120 Church Street* 8/6/97
REAL ESTATE WEEKLY *New Housing Type Emerges from Downtown Conversions* 6/25/97
NEW YORK TIMES *Conversions Are Brisk in Downtown Manhattan* 5/30/97
NEW YORK TIMES *Provincetown Playhouse Being Restored by NYU* 4/30/97
INTERIORS *A Wonderful Thing Happened on 57th Street* 8/96
NEW YORK TIMES *Former Insurance Tower to Have 437 Apartments* 7/21/96
REAL ESTATE WEEKLY *Who's News: MMA Merger* 4/3/96
NEW YORK TIMES *Silent Tower on 10th is Coming Back to Life* 7/30/95
CRAIN'S *Small Business Veterans Award* 6/95
ARCHITECTURE *Melrose Court* 4/95
MULTI HOUSING NEWS *Pillars of the Industry Awards '94* 1994
NEW YORK TIMES *From Fake Windows to Real Rehabilitation* 5/22/94

NEW YORK TIMES *At Melrose Court, Progress in Shades of Teal* 5/8/94
NEW YORK TIMES *20 Abandoned Buildings Being Restored in the Bronx* 1/3/92
NEW YORK TIMES *Higher Density Goal Spurs New Designs* 11/10/91
LITCHFIELD TIMES *Washington Man's Projects Help Shelter the Homeless* 4/13/90
DAILY NEWS *'A New Start' for Homeless* 11/7/89
REAL ESTATE WEEKLY *Ceremony Celebrates Opening of Bronx Homeless Housing* 9/13/89
THE WESTSIDER *There's a Home in Their Future* 9/89
NEW YORK CONSTRUCTION NEWS *Bids Out Next Week for 20-Building Rehabilitation Project in the Bronx* 8/7/89
REAL ESTATE WEEKLY *'Sledging Marks' Start of Bronx Housing Rehab* 7/26/89
NEW YORK POST *Seeking 42,000 for South Bronx* 7/20/89
NEW YORK TIMES *Fake Window Decals Pulled In Favor of Real Occupants* 7/12/89
NEW YORK TIMES *New Rochelle Condos* 7/86
IMPACT *Greencroft Condos Underway in New Rochelle* 6/18/86
NEW YORK CONSTRUCTION NEWS *Summer Construction Set For New Rochelle Condo* 4/14/86
TOMORROW *Greencroft Condos Under Construction* 4/7/86
REAL ESTATE WEEKLY *Suburbia: a More Sophisticated Approach* 2/3/86
UNKNOWN SOURCE *'Tile' Condos Add Color to Skyline in New Rochelle* 1986
NEW YORK TIMES *Fitting a 'Sliver' Building Into the Block* 5/18/84
ENR *Firm Attracts Foreign Partners* 3/10/83
REAL ESTATE WEEKLY *Innovative Interior Design Will Play a Major Marketing Role* 3/7/83
REAL ESTATE WEEKLY *'Trust' Is Essential When Dealing With Foreign Partners Says Fallis* 2/14/83
THE STAR-LEDGER *Foreigners 'bet' on Britton's Track Record* 1/21/83
REAL ESTATE WEEKLY *From Start to Finish* 12/6/82
REAL ESTATE WEEKLY *New Interiors Enhance Historic Facades* 11/22/82
NEW YORK POST *Historic Townhouses Restored Inside & Out* 11/12/82
THE STAR-LEDGER *Britton Chief Says Developers Have to Mend Their Ways* 11/12/82
REAL ESTATE WEEKLY *"Full Service" Means More Than Ever According to Britton Development* 9/8/82
NEW YORK TIMES *Methodically, Small Developer Expands in Manhattan* 10/16/81
HOUSE AND GARDEN REMODELING GUIDE *A Lakeside Cabin Grows* Fall/Winter 1979
HOUSE AND GARDEN DECORATING GUIDE *An Addition Triples Living Space for Year-Round Vacations* Fall 1979
HOUSE AND GARDEN *Planned for Children* Fall 1979
RESTAURANT AND HOTEL DESIGN *Solving the Puzzle: New Look for Columbus Avenue* Jan/Feb 1984
NIKKEI ARCHITECTURE *Renovation of an Old Factory: Eight Apartments Around a Courtyard* 3/20/78
ARCHITECTURAL RECORD *High-Density Apartment Conversion in New York City Affords Special Design Amenities* 9/77
ARCHITECTURAL RECORD *Playful Shapes Transform an Old Building With Respect* 11/75
ARCHITECTURAL RECORD *Architecture for Preschoolers: Up From the Jungle Gym* 5/75
ARCHITECTURAL RECORD *Play is Not a Negative Educational Pursuit* 5/75
ARCHITECTURAL RECORD *Schools That Nurture an Understanding for the Dimensions of Life* 5/75
ST. PAUL SUNDAY PIONEER PRESS *Classrooms Sculptured to Child's World* 4/6/75

BETTER HOMES AND GARDENS *Nursery School Co-op: A Design to Delight Small Fry* 3/75
FRANKLIN'S ALMANAC *Those We Help: Bank Loan Gives 90 Preschoolers an Innovative Learning Environment* 3/74
NEWSDAY *Their Classroom is a Toy to Behold* 12/7/73

Books:
Design For Living: Affordable Family Housing
"Good Neighbors"
Jones, Pettus, Pyatok
Images Publishing 1997
Guest Speaker: The Dalton School

Lectures & Seminars:
Breathing New Life Into Existing Structures
"Converting White Elephants into Derby Winners"
Build Boston
Boston Society of Architects
November 1997

Expanding the Architect's Role In Affordable Housing
American Institute of Architects Housing
PIA
October 1997

Future Vision of Urban Public Housing
An International Forum, University of Cincinnati
College of Design, Architecture, Art and Planning
November 1994

Radio Interview, WNYC Radio
February 10, 1983

Lecturer and Exhibitor, Mind, Child, Architecture
A Conference Celebrating the International Year of the Child
Rutgers University
Newark, NJ
October 1979

Guest Presenter, Dedication of New Play Environment
Great Neck Child Development Center
Great Neck, NY
May 1976

Montessori Concerns: Moral Competence in Young Children and Learning Disabilities
Seminar, Boston College
Boston, Massachusetts
June 1974